Returning to College, Continuing to Learn, After 50

Stories of 15 Individuals Who Made a College Comeback and a Commitment to Lifelong Learning

By Susan Sarver

NEW FORUMS

NEW FORUMS PRESS INC.

Published in the United States of America
by New Forums Press, Inc.1018 S. Lewis St.
Stillwater, OK 74074
www.newforums.com

Copyright © 2017 by New Forums Press, Inc.

Library of Congress Cataloging-in-Publication Data Pending

This book may be ordered in bulk quantities at discount from New Forums
Press, Inc., P.O. Box 876, Stillwater, OK 74076 [Federal I.D. No. 73 1123239].
Printed in the United States of America.

ISBN 10: 1-58107-302-X
ISBN 13: 978-1-58107-302-7

Table of Contents

Acknowledgements

I am grateful to all of the scholars and experts who shared their stories, experiences, and expertise for this collection.

Special thanks to my family and the Writers' Bloc class of the University of Oregon's Osher Lifelong Learning Institute of Central Oregon.

Preface

"The noblest pleasure is the joy of understanding."
– Leonardo da Vinci

I call it the itch—that persistent restlessness to achieve, to know the world more deeply, to learn something new. For me that itch was highly specific. I wanted to go to graduate school.

After more than two decades, I still hadn't outgrown it. In fact, the passage of time and the accumulation of age only seemed to exacerbate it. Then, at age 58, I discovered an opportunity, a balm to relieve the itch: a low residency Master of Fine Arts (MFA) program in creative writing. I applied, gained acceptance, and headed back to school full-time, joining a small cohort of talented students, some of whom were younger than my children.

I was a little intimidated at first, but I was also ecstatic. Suddenly reading and studying took priority over pitching freelance features, pulling weeds, and doing laundry. I confess the whole thing felt rather self-indulgent, but I quickly got over that feeling. For what a joy it was to embark on a new academic challenge and to give focused time and effort to gaining a new body of knowledge, exchanging ideas with faculty and students, and rediscovering the sense of hope that goes along with getting a new degree. I wanted this graduate experience, this degree so badly it never occurred to me that at some point during the next two years, I might have moments of doubt and at times, I would even question my decision to return to school. How I wish I'd had this book tucked into my backpack to help me through these moments.

This work aspires simply to offer a small collection of inspiring stories from individuals who became students again after age 50 and others who continue to make learning a vital part of their lifestyle. The volume is divided into two sections. The first features nine professionals who returned to college life after age 50 to obtain new degrees. Here is a virtual community of people who generously share their insights on navigating academia as an older student. The second section presents six lifelong learners who have made continued study a way of life through widely varied approaches. I count myself a member of both of these groups, the return-to-schoolers as well as the lifelong learners, and I include pieces of my own story here and there as well.

When I first considered how to approach a book on returning to school and continuing to learn after age 50, I knew immediately I wanted to focus on the stories of those who had done it. I wanted to talk to individuals who overcame extraordinary obstacles, made bold moves from good jobs and comfortable lifestyles, and honored their plans and their hearts, even amid criticism, in order to return to school again and to follow their learning dreams. After each and every one of my conversations with these scholars, I felt newly energized and freshly inspired. I conducted the interviews for this collection between fall 2015 and spring 2016, which means the stories and ages of the individuals represent a snapshot in time.

Though I also interviewed several experts as well, who kindly shared knowledge and insights based on their particular expertise as it relates to later-in-life academic pursuits, the expertise that forms this work is rooted in experience. I have a deep respect for experience as a fine and at times, scrappy educator that extends back to childhood. My dad liked to say that he got his education in the School of Hard Knocks. For a long time, I thought it strange he'd gone to a college that expected its students to use brute knuckle force to enter its halls. Eventually, I caught on to what he meant. When he'd first entered the industrial world, he was a farmer who hadn't gone to college but needed to support a family of seven. He was a hard worker, good with people, and he quickly made his way up to executive status in the auto industry. Eventually, he was running the place. In time, he took a few college classes based on his need to know the subject, but he never felt the need to add official academic credentials to his name. Yet, he was one of the smartest people I've ever known. He was a living illustration of experience and its invaluable role in learning. Of course, I also have the greatest respect for scholarship and research, hallmarks of higher education. But human stories have a way of seeping into our hearts and enduring. An example of the power and potential of story as educator that I remain in awe of is Stud's Terkel's *Working*. That remarkable collection of stories of individual work experiences still has much to teach us about the nature of work.

While this collection focuses on learners over the age of 50, these stories are likely to resonate with non-traditional students of any age. And for anyone who wants to go back to school but hesitates, particularly because they believe they are too old, encouragement can be found here. You are not alone. Plenty of older students all over the country are hitting the books again. According to the National Center for Education Statistics, in the fall of 2013, more than 700,000 students over age 50 were enrolled in degree-granting, post-secondary institutions (https://nces.ed.gov/programs/digest/d14/tables/dt14_303.50.asp).

The lifelong learners presented in the second section exude a kind of collective joy in pursuing new knowledge and skills. These scholars bring an inventive independence to learning that is refreshing, yet they are no less driven than those who chose to go back to college for a new degree.

Research findings regularly make headlines, reconfirming the benefits of continuing to challenge the mind by learning throughout the lifespan. Thus, the world has come to embrace continued learning as vital to optimal health and aging well. While these perks for the mind might not be the primary reason for returning to school and living the learning life, it is comforting to know that the effort of taking on new learning challenges later in life provides payoffs beyond a sense of personal achievement, a deeper understanding of the world, and the simple joy of acquiring new knowledge.

When I interviewed Margery Silver, Ed.D., and learned about her work as associate director of the New England Centenarian Study (NECS), I was particularly delighted to hear her personal reaction to the scientific discoveries she and her colleagues had made. "Talk about a new lease on life," she said. "It gave you the sense that there was so much more to come ... When you think about what is happening with the lifespan, at 50 you're only about half-way there." When I heard this, I got a sense of time unfolding with hope and possibility. I had a similar feeling after talking with each of the extraordinary people who shared their experiences for this project.

I am in awe of and humbled by the individuals who shared their stories for this collection. Their educational experiences tell the deeper and broader story of learning after 50. I invite readers to find in them, as I have, encouragement, hope, and inspiration to keep on learning.

Chapter 1
Thinking it Through

"Deep into that darkness peering, long I stood there, wondering, fearing,
Doubting, dreaming dreams no mortal ever dared to dream before;"
— excerpt from *The Raven* by Edgar Allen Poe

The higher education messaging I grew up on was brief and to the point: get in, get what you need to get a good job, and get out as quickly and cheaply as possible. I honored those expectations by grabbing an associate of arts degree in nursing, passing the boards, becoming licensed, and getting a job as a registered nurse before turning 20. Eventually, I rebelled.

The first time I headed back to school as a non-traditional student was to pursue a bachelor's degree in English. At that time, my children were young and life was chaotic. I dressed in the dark, fed the kids, saw the older child off to school by bus, dashed across town to get the younger one to preschool, then drove back across town in an attempt to make my 9 a.m. classes. I was always late. One morning as I discreetly slipped into a back-row seat, I looked down at my feet to discover I was wearing running shoes of two different colors. Despite the challenges of keeping it all together, the chance to sit quietly in that classroom and put something new into my brain was blissful. I was sure that becoming a non-traditional college student at the age of 58 would be quite a different experience than it was in my thirties. Though my brain was a couple of decades older, to my surprise, returning to school this time was far easier. With fewer family responsibilities and more time to study, it was a much more enjoyable learning experience. I also was much more aware of what a privilege it was to be attending college again in the fifth decade of my life. To be honest, I was actually rather surprised to be accepted into a graduate program at an age that is more than twice what the National Center for Education Statistics considers the youngest age (24) of the non-traditional student. I was thrilled. However, when I allowed my enthusiasm to spill over in a moment of sharing with a neighbor of comparable vintage the news of my latest academic venture, he looked at me incomprehensively as if I had just announced I was expecting twins.

The reasons for returning to school later in life are as complex and unique as the individual. For some, it is a critical path to fulfilling a lifelong dream. For others, the chance to pursue a new degree might simply be a gift to the self or perhaps it's the means to ignite hope for the future and a renewed enthusiasm for life. The decision to go back to school might have emotional or psychological roots such as a wife and mother who feels alienated from her family after her husband and children have successfully achieved graduate and professional degrees. Going back to school might well be the means to destroy lifelong barriers erected by parents who didn't value or encourage learning beyond the basics. The main motivation could be entirely practical and tied to hopes of expanding career opportunities or cross training to prepare for a new position, or of developing a hybrid work situation that merges two different disciplines. Others might crave the intellectual challenges of a structured program or desire to remain scholarly engaged—to delve deep into social, political, and environmental issues of the past and present through academic discussion and research. Some might be on an outright mission to get the degree required to give back in a specific way or to meet a need within the community or to relieve a desire they've spent a lifetime denying, even going so far as to commit to the long haul of obtaining a medical or law degree. Still others might wish to go back to school simply for the joy of learning.

Whatever the reason, becoming a student again will surely stimulate new ways of thinking and generate ideas that might never be discovered without the intellectual trigger of a formal learning environment. Acquiring a fresh layer of knowledge could reveal entrepreneurial interests or sift to the surface an interest in writing, painting, or music that is no longer content to be shoved aside by life's more pressing duties, or it might even expose a previously unrecognized skill or talent. The potential for personal reward and discovery is significant and can continue to unfold years after completing a course of study. Going to school at any age is a life adventure, and no one can predict what might come of it either during the process or after completing it.

Individual circumstances can bear heavily on the back-to-school decision and the studying experience at any age. Returning to school full time to obtain an entirely new undergraduate degree might collide sharply with a spouse's idea of retirement plans that involve settling in together on the sofa to view a library of movies accumulated over the past 40 years. Meshing two disparate desires might take some creative thinking and perhaps a little negotiating. Sorting out the time and financial commitments with a spouse or partner before diving back into a formal academic program can make all the difference in preserving close relationships and avoiding a point of panic midway into a program that sparks the question: "What have I gotten myself into?"

The itch to earn a master's degree struck me in my early thirties, soon after completing a bachelor's degree. It was during a phone conversation with a newspaper editor, just after I'd pitched the idea of working as a stringer. "Go get a masters degree," he said, "then we'll talk." I had been aiming to put forth the kind of effort that generated income rather than working at something that consumed it. But the editor's words got under my skin, almost like an antigen that gave rise to a restless desire to find the right place and time to return to graduate school.

Like pretty much everyone, I had plenty of good reasons to defer the dive back into academia. There were jobs to work, relocations to complete, home renovations to undertake, children to raise and educate, broken cars to repair, surgeries to undergo, a hurricane or two to flee. There was simply no time or space for graduate school and studies. But the itch persisted.

Every now and then I would poke around for programs and graduate school developments and dream about applying to a low-residency MFA program in creative writing, not journalism as Mr. Newspaper Editor had advised. I focused on programs that allowed students to study where they lived and to travel once or twice a year for a weeklong residency of intensive instruction. But I never allowed my dream to carry me so far as to actually get up the courage to apply; and of course, life remained so busy.

Then one day while living in Louisiana, a hurricane called Katrina came along when we least expected it, and it changed us as it did the entire city of New Orleans. We bounced here and there and eventually found our way to the high, dry desert of Central Oregon where I learned of plans to launch a new MFA program. My children were grown and my husband was supportive; I mustered up the nerve to apply. I was sure that my *curriculum vitae* with its work history dating way back to 1975 would get me no farther than the pile of applicants targeted to receive in the mail a sad, thin envelope with a letter of pleasant decline. Instead, I got a call from the director telling me I was accepted. The twenty-plus-year itch finally found relief.

Of course, any individual over 50 with a desire to return to school is also probably the kind of person who likes to look carefully at all facets of the decision and anticipate ahead of time any potentially negative aspects. One of the biggest obstacles to going back to school as an older student might well be fear--the fear of not being smart enough or fast enough or not fitting into contemporary student culture. If decades have passed since the previous segment of formal education, encountering new technologies, new ways of communicating, and new tools for teaching, learning, and testing can be intimidating. This too is part of education even if it is tangential to the curriculum. Colleges and universities commonly offer a plethora of resources and technical support to help students become proficient in using new technology and operating learning tools like Blackboard, Moodle, and Canvas. They can even help students launch blogs and websites.

If the first round or two of higher education wasn't all

that enjoyable, feeling reluctant to return to a similar type of institution is understandable. It might be helpful to consider the circumstances of that less-than-optimal experience. Perhaps the particular program turned out to be a poor fit or the timing was difficult or there were personal issues that posed challenges to studying. Maybe there was an unfair grading system or an egoist professor who enjoyed tricking students and got off on making learning and testing a miserable experience. I will never forget one English professor who required students to type critical essays on paper composed of 25 percent cotton rag. She was a harsh grader, and most of us had our papers returned bloodied with red ink and topped with poor grades, which had to be earned by making all the corrections and revisions perfectly and without making new errors in the process. Failing to do so meant accepting a zero for the assignment. The grading scheme felt like a game that only the professor could win and much of what we learned through this process was fear of making mistakes. Eventually, student grumbling and complaints reached the department chairman, and suddenly, things changed dramatically. Despite that unfortunate experience, I never regretted my decision to return to school, and I definitely felt a special bond of suffering with my fellow students, despite being older.

After more than ten years of working in higher education, I am convinced that administrators are taking student feedback more seriously. Informal online venues, such as RateMyProfessors.com, give students an additional platform to be heard in ways that were unfathomable a couple of decades ago. Of course, every academic experience is unique and what was unpleasant about school at age 20 might not make the same impact at age 55. On the other hand, if dancing to classmates' karaoke singing was a blast back in your twenties, as a sixty-year-old, this type of mandatory fun might be more of a socially awkward time-eater. Time changes us; however, the experience gained through decades of living provides personal resources for managing and coping with less-than-perfect academic scenarios.

Blending faculty and students, both of whom might be of

widely varying ages with diverse professional experiences, can give rise to interesting interactions. Some prospective back-to-schoolers might have concerns about studying with younger instructors who could easily be around the ages of children or even grandchildren. It can be humbling to discover that your professor is the same age as your granddaughter yet has professional experiences consistent with someone three times her age. However, the opposite scenario is also possible: older students, particularly those pursuing coursework in areas in which they have or are currently working, might discover they have more professional experience than the instructor. The great thing about being a student is there's no obligation to share such a fact. Faculty are hired for their expertise, and approaching the learning process with an open mind, a bit of humility, and a willingness to learn from everyone—even from fellow students—maximizes the opportunities to absorb all that formal education has to offer. More thoughts on this in chapter six.

There might be similar concerns about relating to a younger student population or looking and feeling like the grandparent in a particular class. If such differences cause so much discomfort they interfere with learning, looking at other options, such as online coursework, might be the way to go.

I'll admit to feeling both excitement and a bit of apprehension about meeting my MFA student cohort at the very first ten-day residency, especially since writing workshops often require close, extended interactions. The additional concern about meeting this group was the context—not only did residency involve learning together, it also meant living together, dorm-style, complete with shared bathrooms--for ten whole days. To my surprise, it turned out three out the eight students were over 50. Though the other five were younger, it simply didn't matter. We were all just writers. And in the heat of discussions and casual chats over our shared passion, age wasn't much of an issue. We all entered the program to become better at our chosen art—and that's a lot of common ground.

I suspected I would be older than nearly all of my faculty

members, which turned out to be the case. One professor, who served as one of my fiction mentors, happened to be the same age as one of my children. But I never really gave the age issue much thought because she is such a brilliant woman and an extraordinary teacher of writing and revision. I felt only gratitude to have had the opportunity to study with such a talented individual, an experience that proved invaluable to my work in fiction.

Family opposition to returning to school could pose a major hurdle. Committing time, money, and attention to academic work without the support and understanding of family members who are still living with you is a set-up for unhappiness all around. But if you're inspired to go back to school, having a serious conversation with those opposed might help them to understand the depth of your desire and the potential for a new academic achievement to positively influence the rest of your life could make all the difference. It might mean asking those in doubt to extend support in the form of a series of gifts that substitute for tangible ones that you usually receive from them on special occasions throughout the year and requesting that the arrangement extend throughout the entire program. Support and understanding of a family member require no wrapping paper, and they make far better gifts than years' worth of gadgets, gizmos, and bad shirts.

To be sure, there are many ways to fulfill the yearning for learning that do not involve a degree-seeking effort at a college or university. Some of these are presented in chapter 15. The possibilities for learning something new in a way that suits individual learning styles and needs are certainly broad and abundant.

In sorting out the pros and cons of choosing either a formal or an informal path of learning, it helps to consider goals, motivations, circumstances, and of course, personal interest and passion. What course of study is most appealing at this stage of life? Will the knowledge gained further a professional goal or objective? Will the decision to return to school or other coursework impact others and how will it affect retirement plans? If the goal is to enhance work opportunities in a current position or to switch jobs entirely, a formal program within a college or university that leads to a certificate or additional degree might be the perfect choice. However, rarely are there guarantees in the job market, and it's wise to consider the costs of the program compared to any potential payoff, factoring in the number of years you plan to continue working.

For some post-50 potential back-to-schoolers, the idea of retirement is volunteering or continuing to work but in an encore career that involves serving the community. Locating specific work and volunteer opportunities, knowing how and where to find them, and determining the specific needs for additional education can be challenging. I asked Doug Dickson, Chair of the Encore Boston Network (http://www.encorebostonnetwork.org/) to share his thoughts on these types of post-retirement careers.

Harnessing the knowledge, skills, experiences, and energy of older adults to help address the wide-range of societal challenges we currently face is the focus of the encore movement (www.encore.org), says Dickson. The organization was founded for purposes of bringing together community leaders, organizations, advocates, and others who care about the idea of expanding work and volunteer opportunities and building connections. Dickson has been involved with the network in various capacities for about fifteen years. He is working to grow the movement so individuals who have an interest in social purpose work at this phase of life can connect with organizations and programs in need of their contributions. "There are, of course, individuals who are finding their way through existing programs," he says. They determine their own needs for certain educational credentials or skill development. But, he says, most people don't know about the opportunities out there and even if they do, they might have to knock on a dozen doors to find out about ones that are a good fit.

In an effort to boost connections, in the fall of 2015, the group organized an encore expo at Boston College, a member of the Boston Encore Network. The event drew a capacity crowd. The attendees included about 30 organizations looking to recruit people to fill significant roles in both volunteer and paid positions.

Other encore efforts are taking place in many cities and the

Encore website lists organizations affiliated with the movement. The AARP (http://www.aarp.org/aarp-foundation/about-us/) offers support as well as information on all sorts of issues of interest to those over 50 who seek to continue working.

Though it's one thing to connect organizational and social needs with individuals motivated to meet those needs, when it comes to filling skill or learning gaps, Dickson hopes the movement will evolve and achieve a critical mass that will help create new pathways into academic institutions. There have been some successes, says Dickson, and some individual programs incorporate an educational component so individuals committed to an encore career or volunteer position can receive the specific training required for the work. Dickson admits, "There's a bias, a sort of societal thinking about what's possible as people get older. And it can work against older workers." But, he adds, individuals can overcome that bias—particularly individuals who don't allow the stereotype to define them and have taken the initiative to gain skills and credentials to do certain kinds of work.

Whether it's to pursue an encore role or to fulfill a personal mission, for some individuals over 50, going back to school might well be the best or perhaps the only choice. Reaching that decision might be the most challenging part of the process.

Decisions, decisions, and more decisions! Deciding to return to school gives rise to a new category of choices. If the commitment to an entirely new program feels overwhelming or becomes a new reason for insomnia, or if you're simply uncertain as to whether going a new direction is right for you, it might be worthwhile as a preface to submitting university applications to test-drive an online or non-credit course in the field of chosen study. Later in the book, Dr. Clarence Nicodemus describes his experience in doing just that in order to gain relevant experience before applying and committing to a new academic program. In addition, a course that is free from the pressure to earn a grade that ends up on a permanent transcript could be invaluable in exposing any knowledge gaps that can be filled before diving into a full-time, degree-granting program.

Plenty of baccalaureate and graduate programs can be completed entirely online or through self-study. Such program formats might make it easier to balance work and family responsibilities with school demands. However, some people prefer classroom interactions and discussions. These can still occur without being physically present in a classroom through such approaches as real-time chat sessions. Still others prefer a program that requires attendance in person.

Though it might be the least pleasant aspect of going back-to-school, the matter of funding is likely to come up in the course of any serious conversation about returning to school. Students over 50 seeking another degree for personal reasons might not be deeply concerned about the cost of making their wishes come true. But those returning to retrain or redirect a career might be under special emotional and financial pressures to make smart choices. Gary E. Carpenter, CPA, who provides College Planning Services in Syracuse, New York, says individuals over 50 should take a serious look at how much they can afford to pay and borrow and suggests exploring options that can give you more bang for the buck. "Take a look at the in-state, public institutions. They can give you some fantastic value for your money," says Carpenter. In addition, many community colleges allow students over 65 to enroll in classes cost-free or at greatly reduced costs. Online degrees are also worth looking at to compare costs. Some employers offer retraining support or special tuition assistance/reimbursement programs, such as the Starbucks College Achievement Plan (https://news.starbucks.com/collegeplan).

The U.S. Department of Education Federal Student Aid website (https://studentaid.ed.gov/sa/resources#funding) offers loads of information on thousands of grants and scholarships; it even has a section on avoiding scams. The possibility of a tax break is also worth investigating at (https://www.irs.gov/uac/tax-benefits-for-education-information-center).

When the return to school is intended to extend work years, it is important to compare the tuition costs with any potential gain in future income. There are online formulas for crunching the numbers and those might be a good place to start, says Carpenter. But Carpenter suggests taking a look at cash flow and figuring the amount required for tuition and comparing it to the amount of expected future earnings and consider if you'll work long enough to pay back the cost of the additional education. He urges caution when it comes to student loans. "Too many people say I'll just go borrow the money," says Carpenter. We've had historically low interest rates but they are likely to start increasing, and many private student loans are variable, meaning that as interest rates change, they respond accordingly. It's important to stop and look hard at the numbers before making such commitments.

After settling on a program that feels like a good fit, considering a plan for funding, it's still wise to get as much information as possible about the institution and the program before actually applying. Study the program description, the required courses, and the pre-requisites. Ask questions and be realistic. But also know that often the aspects of a program that make it or break it come down to people and personalities. Such human factors can strongly influence the quality of the broader learning experience particularly in a program that requires extended interactions with the same personalities for the duration of the program. Individual departments should have course requirements available online, and the program director or department administration should be able to put you in touch with current students to find out more. However, even with due diligence, there's no way to know every detail and factor that might impact the experience. Even a student currently enrolled in the program might not know or be reluctant to reveal that a specific instructor plays favorites or has issues with older students. There is no way to know everything until you jump in.

Anyone with a will to go back to school will surely find a way to make it happen. It is never too late to become a student, to learn something new and to discover that the process is often as valuable as the end product.

Part I

Going for a Formal Degree

Chapter 2
Clearing Admission Hurdles

"Start by doing what's necessary; then what's possible; and suddenly you are doing the impossible."

— Francis of Assisi

Mark Twain once said, "The secret of getting ahead is getting started. The secret of getting started is breaking your complex overwhelming tasks into small manageable tasks, and starting on the first one." Though not sources agree that Twain was the actual author of this simple truth, the words seem a good fit for the college application process.

Of course, academic programs vary as to specific requirements, which should be accessible on the school's website. Professional schools typically require special entrance exams, such as the MCAT or LSAT. Programs in the arts might request a portfolio, and though not all graduate programs require the GRE, many do. For some older students, particularly those who have been out of school for an extended period of time and haven't taken a standardized test in decades, exam requirements and the expectation to score at a certain level might well prompt a change in plans. Though challenging, testing requirements need not be a deal-killer. Study materials and courses to prepare for such tests are in abundance, and in some instances, the school might make an exception. Here's how two determined students overcame their admission hurdles through creative thinking, perseverance, and grace.

Linda Webb, B.S., aged 67, is finally doing the work she was meant to do: serving as a special education teacher at what she describes as "the best school in the world, Peabody High School in Trenton, Tennessee." Her students have special learning challenges, such as autism and Down Syndrome. Webb often begins her work with them by drafting a list of what they can do and cannot do. The results often surprise the students. "They find out there's more they can do than they can't do," says Webb. She sees certain students who believe they've topped out and cannot make any more progress. Webb speaks with the authenticity of one experienced in overcoming obstacles. She tells them, "You've got to believe in yourself. You don't top out until you're under the ground and through learning." Learning has been a life-changer for Webb. But her path through higher education was a challenging one and the entire journey took place after the age of 50. She was 16 and in her senior year when she decided to quit high school to get married. (She celebrated her 50th wedding anniversary this past year). Her first child came along when she was 20 and the second was born when she was 21. She stayed home to care for the children until they started school then went to work in the garment factory. She started out as a machine operator but over the next 20 years or so, worked her way up to supervisor.

Around the time the country was obsessing over Y2K and the possible implications of rolling into a new century, the garment industry was folding up operations and moving overseas, Webb's employer among them. The company offered her a good position in their new facilities in the Dominican Republic. Webb had been born in Tennessee and lived there all of her life. She also had her family to think about and, by that time, she was helping to raise grandchildren. She declined the offer. Webb admits to indulging in a brief pity party. She was 52 years old with no high school diploma. "I realized I didn't have any skills to get a job. That was all I knew."

Webb wanted more than another job, and she was aware of a government program for displaced workers whose employers moved overseas that provided funding to help pay for college. But she first had to overcome the obstacle of getting a GED. She showed up at a facility that offered GED training and testing, but the class was already in progress and was nearing the end of the term. The instructor acknowledged Webb's work skills and encouraged her to give the test a try anyway. With grandchildren in tow, she sat down, took the test, and passed--at the top of the class. The instructor asked why she wasn't going on to college, and Webb replied that she didn't know how to do anything but work in a garment factory, and she added, "I'm too old."

Webb will never forget the instructor's rebuttal: "Well, how old are you going to be this time next year if you don't go back?" Those words struck a nerve in Webb.

She had been out of school for a long time and couldn't even apply for an education grant until she was tested. But Webb made up her mind to give it a try anyway. But when she showed up at the unemployment office to take the test, the woman in charge looked her up and down as if appraising her age and said to Webb: "Ma'am, you can't pass these tests to get into community college.... Why don't you just go get a job at Walmart?" Webb politely responded. "No, Ma'am. Just bring it on." She took the test and passed.

With the GED behind her, Webb enrolled in Jackson State Community College, signing up for classes in early childhood education with the hope of securing a position in day care or a Head Start program after completing an associate of arts degree. But when she showed up for class, her excitement quickly faded. As she strolled down the halls of her new college carrying a bag from the bookstore bulging with nearly $200 in textbooks, she glanced through the open doors of the classrooms and became aware of a new hitch—every room had a computer. "I didn't even know how to turn a computer on," says Webb. How she overcame this technical knowledge gap is described in chapter eight. Meanwhile, Webb had to address another educational gap. Because she had been out of high school for so many years and had never taken the usual standardized tests, such as ACT, she was required to complete developmental courses in math and English.

Webb dove into the work, quickly checked off the requirements and moved on to the program curriculum.

She attended school as a full-time student, taking no less than 12 to 18 credit hours each semester. At the same time, she cleaned houses and worked a modified second shift at Delta in Jackson, getting off work at 2:30 a.m. to dash home, catch a few hours of sleep, get up at 6:00 a.m. to take grandchildren to school and get herself back to campus. Webb says it was determination and God's help that got her through it.

She also received support from her instructors. "I had some awesome teachers," Webb says. "They were so encouraging." Webb was eager to learn and always sat in the front row. "I had teachers who realized I was there to learn, but I was in a foreign environment." That sense of feeling out of place was related to age, and Webb was keenly aware that one thing her fellow students had that she didn't was time. They were fresh out of high school. They were free. They could do what they wanted. They could take a class over again if necessary. Webb didn't have such luxuries. She told herself, "This is it. This is my shot at doing what I didn't do back then." She recalls the first paper she wrote for her English class. It was an essay about feeling like she was Rip Van Winkle. She turned it in with the comment, "I can't write."

The teacher quickly countered her and responded: "Yes, you can write!"

By the time Webb reached the second semester, she was getting the hang of college work and decided to sneak in some extra courses that weren't part of the requirement, adding upper level classes in special education to her already loaded semesters. The courses confirmed her interest in special education.

In May of 2004, Webb received an Associate of Arts Degree from Jackson State, graduating *Magna Cum Laude.* She went to work as a special education teacher assistant at Milan Middle School in Milan, Tennessee, where her grandchildren went to school. But Webb wanted more. She wanted to become a teacher, not remain an assistant. She discovered another funding opportunity--in the form of an educational grant for an assistant who had already achieved significant academic distinction. Webb was a perfect candidate. She applied and received the award and returned to college studies once again.

Though she didn't have the same difficulties as the first time she attended college, returning to school remained challenging. Webb was working her full-time teaching assistant job while taking a full course load of 12 to 18 credits per semester, opting for night classes and courses online. "There wasn't anything easy about any of it. But if you want it bad enough, you can do it." She completed her Bachelor of Science Degree with an emphasis on special education at Bethel University, graduating *Magna Cum Laude* in December 2007, and began her career as a special education teacher in 2008.

Education is one thing that can't be taken away from you, Webb says. It's a principle she has tried always to pass along to her children and her students as well. She appears to have been successful. The day Webb graduated, her older daughter shared the stage, receiving a nursing degree. Says Webb, "It was one of the happiest moments in my life when we graduated together."

Discovering the requirement to take a standardized test, such as the Graduate Record Examination (GRE) that many graduate schools require or the Graduate Management Admission Test (GMAT), a common prerequisite to apply to programs in business, can pose major barriers for students who have been out of school for a significant period of time. Back when Karen Love, MAG, aged 70, found a graduate program that suited her, she quickly discovered that it came with a scary GRE requirement. Rather than waving the white flag on her plans, she mustered up the courage to ask a few key questions that paid off in a big way.

In her post-graduate role, Love models the active, vibrant life she desires for the members of Community Connections in Greater Midtown Detroit. As the organization's outreach coordinator, she engages community sponsors, service providers, and volunteers to support various programs and activities that promote health and wellness, provide social and educational activities, and help meet the needs of seniors living on fixed and limited incomes. "I look at my seniors as being VIPs—as Very Intelligent People," says Love.

The organization is modeled after the Village to Village movement (http://vtvnetwork.org/), a membership-based effort that supports services and programs that enable seniors to continue living in their homes for as long as possible. "It started out on the East Coast where a group of individuals determined that they wanted to age in place," says Love. "Rather than move out of their community, they wanted to pool resources together and share." Love's life and professional experiences, including more than 30 years working in communications and media, have been invaluable to her efforts to build a network of neighbors helping neighbors. The people she touched within the corporate and broader communities in her previous professional work are often the same people she touches today in her work with Community Connections. "It's a quilt," she says. But Love doesn't rely solely on the connections and skills she developed through a long and illustrious career. She has also worked to build her expertise in the field of gerontology. Three years earlier, at the age of 67, she completed her Master's Degree at the University of Southern California Leonard Davis School Of Gerontology.

Returning to school as an older student was nothing new for Love. She completed all of her college degrees-- a Bachelor Degree of Christian Education from the Eastern North Carolina Theological Institute, and a Bachelor of Science Degree in Sociology—after the age of 50.

Love says, "It's interesting because when I've been asked to speak to individuals, they say, 'you're an inspiration.'" But then she has to explain that her story is not typical. "I had an amazing career before I even went back to school," she says. When she retired after 20 years with the *Michigan Chronicle*, she was the paper's chief operating office. "I did not have the degrees that normally go along with a position like that."

Back when she first entered college immediately after high school, life began to unfold in exciting and unexpected ways. "It was my intention to become a social worker early in my life course," Love says. "I graduated from high school in 1964, spent a semester in a university, then fell in love, and that was it," she says. As she and her husband moved about, she continued to take college classes here and there, and she launched her career without a degree.

"I fell into newspaper back in the '70s," Love says. The couple had relocated to Los Angeles, and she was looking for work. Love knew she could type 70 words a minute, so she wandered down to the *L.A. Times* to inquire as to whether an administrative position might be open. She took an initial screening test for job applicants and failed. But the decision-makers liked the looks of her resume, which was dotted with college courses and loaded with community involvement. They interviewed and hired her that same day. "I guess my spirit just kind of touched them," she says, adding, "I also had some great letters of recommendation." They always help, Love says. "I tell people when I go out to talk to them: make sure you get letters of recommendations. You never know when you're going to need them."

She worked the position for three years before moving to Chicago where she accepted a job with the *Chicago Tribune.* In less than a year, her husband was ready to leave the cold behind and return to California, which might have meant yet another job change for Love. But an interesting opportunity presented itself—one that causes Love to stop and reflect. "I've seen the hand of God in my life for all my life course," she says. "The *Chicago Tribune* needed someone to represent the newspaper on the West Coast. They called me." She became the *Tribune's* regional representative, traveling throughout eleven states.

Eventually, Love returned to Michigan and began a twenty-year career with the *Michigan Chronicle,* ultimately moving up to become the COO. Throughout the years, she received numerous awards for excellence and leadership and served on a wide variety of boards. After retiring from the newspaper in 2009, Love was determined to complete her Bachelor's Degree in Sociology. She had obtained an associate's degree about a decade earlier. Those credits combined with other transferable courses she had taken here and there meant she needed only 45 more credits to complete her undergraduate studies. "I didn't realize I had put that much time in over the years."

Love enrolled in Eastern Michigan University to study sociology. At this point in her life, she was a widow and an empty nester. But she had taken a new full-time position with a non-profit, serving as director of communication and media relations for Detroit Rescue Mission Ministries. She also had obligations to her church ministry. With the exception of one online course, Love's classes all took place on campus, which meant a 45-mile drive at least three times per week. Though there were few students her age, Love was delighted to find the classes to be largely intergenerational. "I absolutely fed on the diversity," she says. "I found that being myself, open, sharing wisdom where needed, worked for me. I actually got a lot of kudos," she says. Love felt that most students simply viewed her as another student pursuing an education, and she even made new friends. "I have a very dear Chaldean friend who is actually younger than my youngest daughter who took me under her wing and tutored me in a math class. I got to know her family very well. We are still very close."

As she neared the end of her undergraduate work, she was already thinking about continuing her studies. "To be honest, the field of gerontology just had a nice ring to it," she says. Love had been raised in an intergenerational home and grew up watching her grandparents care for her great-grandmother who lived to be 107. "The closer I got to graduation and the more conversations I had with my professors, I felt that it would be a good fit, especially with my community background and state involvements." Love had served for a time as a senior brigade officer in the state's office of the attorney general, addressing safety issues for seniors, in addition to spending three terms as a volunteer executive council member of AARP Michigan. When Love graduated in 2011, she made sure her grandchildren were present. "I told them this is something I wanted all my life . . . just to let them know that you never give up on a dream," she says. "I think they got it."

Love started her search for a graduate program in gerontology close to home. Wayne State offered one but awarded a certificate rather than a degree, and it required her to take additional classes prior to applying. "I wanted a degree to hang on the wall," she says. She did some online research and up popped USC's program, listed as the oldest and largest school of gerontology in the world. The program, offered entirely online, was a good fit, except for one thing: the GRE was one of the application requirements. It posed a difficult hurdle, and Love admits, "It kind of frightens you." But she wasn't ready to abandon her plan. She decided to speak with a counselor, explaining that the GRE made her nervous. She described how important it was for her to get this degree because she could fill a lot of slots in a lot of lives of individuals her age and older. The counselor took her message to the board; they agreed to waive the requirement providing she wrote a paper explaining her reasons for wanting the degree and maintained a B average or higher throughout the program. Love's response: "I can show you better than I can tell you." She not only wrote her way out of the GRE, she went on to complete her Masters in gerontology with a 3.4+ GPA.

It is fortunate for the members of Community Connections that Love got her graduate degree in gerontology. She has applied her studies to making a difference in many lives. "The biggest reward is that I am in the field where I'm supposed to be at this time in my life," says Love.

When I applied to the MFA program, I was fortunate to encounter only a few small, unexpected challenges. After reviewing the application requirements considered, I made a "To Do" list and figured the entire process, even factoring in a few potential technical hurdles, would fall on the difficulty scale somewhere between renewing my driver's license and formatting a grant for the National of Institutes of Health. It leaned toward the latter.

I was delighted to discover that I didn't have to face the GRE issue. However, one of the requirements was a writing sample. I pulled of few selections from my portfolio of recent work. The challenge was resisting the urge to speculate which particular genre the decision-makers might favor; the bigger challenge was battling my tendency to edit endlessly.

The fact that so many higher ed application processes have gone online might be convenient or not, depending on individual fondness for technology. But even with online formats designed to streamline the process, completing a university application takes time, organization, and advance planning. Tracking down transcripts, requesting letters of recommendation, and completing forms that ask for facts that might be long forgotten is all normal procedure. Starting the hunting and gathering process early and asking for letters of recommendation as soon as possible helps avoid running up against application deadlines.

I figured the transcript gathering would be one of the easier items on my application To Do list. I ordered and paid for them online, one for my nursing degree and another for my bachelor's degree, requesting they be sent directly to the graduate school. I drew a satisfying line through the "Order transcripts" item on my list. Done! Not long after I'd put that detail out of my mind, I received a letter from the graduate school informing me that I was required to submit transcripts from every college I had ever attended. "Order transcripts" re-appeared on the To Do list.

Though I'd completed my Associate's Degree in Nursing at one college, to complete my B.A. in English, I had pieced together coursework from various colleges and universities during various military moves, which meant contacting each of those institutions for individual transcripts, even if I had taken only one class. Over the course of more than 20 years, I had never found a need to request transcripts from these individual institutions until the grad school application. I was glad I'd made transcript ordering an application priority so I still had plenty of time to place these additional orders and requests.

Letters of recommendation might feel a little awkward to the older student, particularly one who has long been positioned to write such letters for others. But such requests can be uncomfortable for students of any age. After all, you're asking someone to write great things about you using nice words and proper grammar, which seems a bit like asking them to write your biography but including only the good parts, plus there's a deadline. For the older student, there is the additional possibility of needing to explain the decision to return to school at this point in life to someone who might think it's a little crazy. Of course, any person that questions the wisdom of your decision might not the right person to ask for a recommendation.

My MFA application required three letters of recommendation. It so happened that the person who best knew my work and was most familiar with the project I hoped to advance through the program stepped forth without being asked and offered to write one of the letters. I was thrilled, but there was one problem: the person offering to write the letter was my older daughter. A fine writer and smart editor, my daughter had listened for years to my stories, essays, columns, and features—anything I wrote and was willing to read aloud to her. But I suspected a letter of recommendation written by a family member to support admission to graduate school would simply be out of the question. But I was so touched by this special offer I decided to ask the program director anyway. To my great surprise, she said 'yes;' she would consider such a letter. The approval transformed the obligatory application process for me, making it deeply personal and entirely memorable.

When it comes to letters, it's good to keep one characteristic of human nature in mind when making the request: people have varying approaches to meeting deadlines. It's always best to give people as much time as possible. Only one out of the three of my letters gave me angst and prompted a gentle text reminder. In the end, the letter arrived in plenty of time and my hours of worry would have been better spent polishing my writing sample.

There are plenty of ways to keep documents organized. My approach was to create an electronic folder on my computer in which to drop completed forms, documents, notes, and writing samples. This made it easy to click and link each document to the online application page. Finally, after I had gathered, reviewed, edited, and re-reviewed all the documents, I loaded them into the online application form, and clicked "submit." Then, tried to forget about it.

Of course, the application was on my mind daily. What if I

missed a document, had a misspelling, or goofed on some gram-mar? What if the decision-makers didn't like my writing, my background, or the fact that, as evidenced by the dates on my *c.v.,* I was an older applicant? Though I very much wanted the gradu-ate degree and the chance to learn again, I knew if I got turned down, I would probably feel sad for a while, but it wouldn't keep me from writing. Life would go on.

Chapter 3

Rising Above Rejection

"Failure is, in a sense, the highway to success..."
– John Keats

Few of us reach the age of 50 without at least a few personal and professional rejections. In some fields of work, such as writing, rejection is so common it simply is part of doing business within the world of publishing. Over the course of many years, I've often encountered a couple of pieces of good advice about managing rejection: don't take it personally and persistence often pays off. I discovered the wisdom in these words while building a file of rejections that grew plump on the road to becoming a published writer

I thought I was reasonably good at handling rejection until I heard the inspiring story of Jody Stubler, FNP-C, aged 64. She not only refused to give into rejection, she used it, dialing-up her goals just a little higher.

About four years ago, Stubler, of Salt Lake City, was busy working two jobs: teaching nursing students and working as a school nurse. The sick children she saw coming to school day-to-day opened her eyes to the unmet healthcare needs in her own community. A surprising number of them never went to the doctor because their families lacked insurance and didn't have the money to pay out-of-pocket fees. At the time, two of her own children lacked health insurance, and they often turned to Stubler to help determine whether or not her grandchildren were sick enough to warrant a visit to a doctor. While she could offer her professional recommendation, she lacked the credentials to diagnose and pre-scribe. Stubler became increasingly aware that it was more than just the children who were affected; entire families were in need. There is something wrong with the system when people can't go to a doctor, says Stubler. She made up her mind to do something about it: to establish the kind of clinic that was missing in her community. That decision, however, meant returning to school to become a family nurse practitioner (FNP).

When Stubler began applying to programs, she was approaching her sixtieth birthday, but that didn't trouble her. "I was kind of a late bloomer anyway," she says. "I didn't even go to college until I was 34." Back then, she had plans of becoming a dietician, but when she discovered how much she enjoyed patient care, she switched to the nursing program at the University of Utah. "It took me seven years to get my Bachelor of Nursing Degree," she says. After graduating, she worked as a registered nurse for a number of years then returned to school again in her mid-fifties to get a Masters Degree in Nursing Education.

She enjoyed teaching, and it was convenient that the school of nursing in which she worked offered a FNP program. She submitted her application, and soon a letter arrived. When Stubler opened it, she was shocked. The school, her own employer, had rejected her. Of small consolation was the invitation to reapply the following year. But waiting another year to start the application process all over again wasn't acceptable, and Stubler set her sights on a program at Georgetown University.

People warned her that Georgetown was one of the hardest schools in the country to get into; some said she would never get accepted. Even one of the school's counselors informed her that it was expensive, competitive, and the acceptance rate was only about ten percent. But Stubler was determined. "Any time you challenge me, I'm going to make it happen," she says.

The application document was around 15 pages long and required responses in essay format. Applicants were also required to submit a video explaining their reasons for wanting to attend Georgetown and how their plans aligned with the school's mission and values. Stubler's video included her intention to open a clinic for uninsured and low-income families after graduation. Georgetown accepted her.

Fast forward to 2014; at the age of 62, Stubler graduated

from Georgetown with honors. (Details of her academic experiences unfold in subsequent chapters. First, there's a clinic to launch and a few more hurdles to clear.)

Armed with her new credentials, Stubler went to work on her plan. She had always envisioned a school-based clinic to provide her services. But when she formally presented the idea, the school district was not interested and declined the offer.

Again, Stubler was not discouraged. She decided to set up her own clinic, one that operated under a different model. But first, she needed a business plan. She asked her son to recommend someone with the background and knowledge to put one together. But her son reminded her that she had just graduated from one of the best schools in the nation and suggested she write the plan. Thus began another segment of Stubler's educational path, one with a steep learning curve. Looking back on it, she says, "It was the greatest learning experience ever."

But before she wrote the plan or looked into a loan, she spotted the perfect property for a clinic. Stubler was willing to pay $110,000. But with a list price of $129,000, the realtor told her the seller would never take it. "We'll come up with a number that'll work for them," Stubler responded. Meanwhile, her husband pointed out all the work that needed to be done on the property to make it suitable for patients. But Stubler saw only the property's potential and was determined to make it happen.

She tapped into her network of friends and acquaintances. She first contacted a banker she knew who invited her to submit the yet-to-be-written business plan when it was ready. Then she prepared an initial draft and sent it to some key people for review--her accountant and her close friend whose husband was a financial planner. Their detailed critiques sent her back to the drawing board. She continued to research and talk to people who had been in business for themselves. She consulted others who had experience running a clinic, a physician who had been in business for himself in two different practices and a surgeon/friend also in private practice. Some advised her not to do it. "I said thanks for the advice, but I'm doing it anyway," Stubler says.

Three months and 51 pages later, Stubler had a business plan for the Hope Family Medical Center. She wrote into the plan a maximum of $115,000 to purchase the property; it was a figure the seller accepted. She got a loan, cashed in her 401K, and added savings to top off her personal financial contribution to the project at $100,000. Most importantly, the plan for the clinic reflected Stubler's professional values. She was all too aware of the corporate tendency to push doctors and nurse practitioners to see as many patients as possible. A patient goes in a room and five minutes later has a prescription and is out the door again, says Stubler. "It's the in-and-out burger mentality of medical care. You cannot diagnose in five minutes. I want to spend time with my patients." Stubler also did not want outside agencies dictating whom she could see and not see. "I did not want to be beholden to insurance companies or government plans that would tell me how to run my business," says Stubler. Consequently, she does not accept insurance. Her model makes healthcare affordable and allows for a meager profit.

On March 16, 2015, the Hope Family Medical Center (http://hopefmc.org/) opened its doors for business. I went through an amazing journey, says Stubler. People often asked if she would do it again, and Stubler answers: "In a heartbeat. I jumped through a million hoops just to graduate, and I graduated with honors. And if I can do that, I can jump through a million more hoops just to open my own clinic."

The commitment, determination, hard work, enthusiasm, and persistence that allowed Stubler to glide past rejection and thrive in a tough academic program continue to serve her well.

Chapter 4

Pushing Past Critics

"Criticism is something we can avoid easily by saying nothing, doing nothing, and being nothing."

– Aristotle

Ideally, announcing your post-50 academic plans to friends and family will generate enthusiasm and encouragement. But that's not always the case. While negative comments might well be rooted in genuine concern, such comments shake your confidence and stir doubt. Staying the course amid criticism calls for courage and determination. Stephanie Manriquez's story illustrates the rewards that can come from staying strong and carrying on. She managed to remain true to herself and her academic plans even amid the abundant and significant concerns of a few critics who are near and dear to her heart.

Stephanie Manriquez, LMT, aged 68, recently retired from her position as director of the massage therapy program at the Central Oregon Community College (COCC) in Bend, Oregon. However, before she could get too comfortable with having extra time, the school invited her back to teach part-time. She accepted the invitation and currently teaches one class online while maintaining her home-based massage therapy business. She is so at ease in these dual roles, it seems as if she's been doing them all of her life. But Manriquez's entire college education and the careers that followed all unfolded after the age of 50.

In 1998, she quit her job, moved to Central Oregon, and went back to school. Some people thought she had lost her mind. She was living in Tacoma at the time and had a great job working as a service tech for a baking supply company, a position that involved traveling throughout the U.S. and abroad. The job even offered some creative perks. While working in the cake decorating division, she helped research and create the edible image, a system for adding a picture to a cake. But as she approached her 50th birthday, Manriquez did some soul searching. "I asked myself a question. If I could do anything I wanted and time and money didn't matter, what did I want to be? I came up with massage therapist." That realization gave rise to new questions. Manriquez missed Central Oregon, where she had lived previously, and began her search for answers there. It just so happened COCC had launched a massage program the previous year. She made a call to a friend who had a spare room to rent. She quit her position with the baking company, moved back to Bend, Oregon, and took a job working at Starbucks. "My kids all thought I was on drugs or had lost my mind," she says. A lot of her friends had the same reaction, wondering how she could give up a secure job with a good paycheck to go off and start over. But Manriquez didn't see it that way. She figured worst-case scenario, she could go back to her old job. "I didn't see the risk. I only saw the potential. I liked different challenges."

Manriquez had lots of experience handling life challenges. She married her high school sweetheart at age 18, and the couple settled in San Juan Capistrano where they had both grown up. They soon had two children and adopted a third. Now and then her husband talked about the possibility of relocating the family to Bend, Oregon. But before those plans came to fruition, her husband was killed in a truck accident. They had been married for nine years. Manriquez remarried within a year, hoping life would be wonderful again. To gain some distance from the memories, she and her new husband moved to Bend, and in time, they had two children. But things were not wonderful, and her second marriage soon came to end.

Single with five children to support, Manriquez created a job for herself by starting a diaper service. She took a second job decorating cakes in a local grocery store. Though cake decorating is something many a mother has mastered, she quickly discovered that completing 10 to 12 cakes a day was a different kind of challenge; but she was motivated, organized, and learned quickly. Eventually, a sixth child came to live with the family most of the time. Life was chaotic, and Manriquez decided to sell the diaper service and focus on raising her family and decorating cakes. She did a fine job and was encouraged to apply for a new opportunity with a baking company. She accepted that position, which took her to Tacoma, saw her through years of raising her family, and brought her to the brink of turning 50 and the realization that she wanted to do something different.

Despite the concern of family and friends, Manriquez followed her heart. She moved back to Central Oregon and enrolled in the one-year massage program at COCC, with the ultimate goal of obtaining her license to practice and setting up her own massage therapy business. She wasn't without her own fears. It had been 32 years since she graduated from high school. As an older student, she wondered how she would be received. She was pleasantly surprised. The average age of the school's student population was early thirties, and in the classroom, no one seemed to care about age. All that was important was the desire to learn and comprehend the material, she says.

"Working at Starbucks helped too," says Manriquez. "All of my supervisors and people I worked with were half my age." Often while sweeping the floor or wiping tables, she noticed customers watching her with looks of pity as if feeling sorry for the poor, old lady having to work at Starbucks. "They didn't know that I was having the time of my life," Manriquez says. "I had no responsibilities. I just had to show up and do my work, and I was going to school. I got paid. I even got a free pound of coffee every week. It was wonderful." Starbucks offered medical insurance for part-time employees, and the company was willing to work with her class schedule. Manriquez had always had a lot of responsibilities in her younger years, so having an opportunity to go after one of her personal goals was exciting. No one in her family had ever obtained a college degree. "When I was growing up, although I took college prep courses, no one ever said, you can go to college. No one ever said, have you thought about doing this?" Instead, "It was get married, have kids, and that's all you did," she says. "Coming back when I was 50 just opened so many doors. It was like, oh my gosh, I could do this, I could do that."

After completing the one-year massage therapy program at the college, Manriquez signed up to take the state board exam to gain licensure and begin practicing. The first part of the test, the written portion, resulted in only half of her class of 16 students passing. The odds of passing the second part of the test proved even worse. It required demonstrating the application of techniques on the body and responding to questions, an approach that was highly subjective based on the interests, background, and whim of the individual examiner. Only one student in class passed, but it wasn't Manriquez. The lone successful licensee was an experienced therapist who had been practicing in another state and sought licensure in Oregon. Knowing that not all states had such regulatory requirements made the experience even more painful.

Manriquez retook the exam, became licensed, and opened her own business, but she believed the testing process was unfair, and she was committed to doing something to change it. She drafted a proposal urging the State Board of Massage Therapists to implement a written standardized test based on an existing national exam that underwent regular, periodic review. Her document carefully outlined all the steps that needed to be taken and why. Some members of the board took offense at the proposed changes. The skills she drew on to make her case confirmed for Manriquez the importance of a good education. As she worked to change things at the state level, Manriquez built her massage therapy practice and she continued to study: this time for an Associates Degree in applied sciences.

After nearly two years and with a little help from a supportive board member, her efforts to sway the group to change testing procedures paid off. Manriquez was pleased. "It showed me what you can do when you get involved and being involved means you need to have an education, you need to be able to speak." Her efforts had put her in touch with a lot of people at the national level of massage therapy oversight and her regulatory involvement deepened. Eventually, she became a member of the Oregon Board of Massage Therapists, serving in the role for eight years.

In 2000, just as she completed her Associates Degree, Manriquez began teaching in the same program from which she had graduated, all the while maintaining her massage therapy business. In the course of teaching, students and prospective students often approached her with their doubts and fears about getting into and through the program. At such times, Manriquez turned her experience into encouragement, telling them, "If I can do it, you can too."

Meanwhile, the college moved the program from the category of continuing education to a credit-based curriculum and Manriquez was encouraged to apply to be its next director. She got the position. Life was full and busy. After getting settled in for a couple of years, Manriquez says, "I thought as long as I'm here, I might as well go ahead and get a bachelor's." In 2002, she started working on her new academic goal: pursuing a degree in business and psychology by taking one class at a time through Eastern Oregon University.

In 2012, ten years later, at the age of 65, Manriquez completed her bachelor's degree. Because she was already enjoying so much career success, some wondered what she was going to do with the new degree. But it was another goal fulfilled for Manriquez; plus, she wanted to hang her diploma on a wall to encourage others in her family to go to college. Many of them have taken the hint. Meanwhile, Manriquez had high expectations for the program she was directing, and she began working to gain full accreditation by the Commission on Massage Therapy Accreditation. She succeeded prior to retiring, another goal accomplished.

Those who once worried about Manriquez leaving job security behind to go off and study massage therapy got a lesson in courage and having faith in yourself. "They're proud of me now," says Manriquez. "People say, 'you're so spontaneous.'" But, she says, "I'm not spontaneous. I think about things a lot, but I don't bounce it off everybody because that just confuses everything. I need to work it out myself, look at what's the good part, what's the bad part … I say I'm irresponsibly responsible."

Chapter 5

Juggling School, Family, Life

"A juggler's skill hath been long years alearning."

– Martin Farquhar Tupper

The Association for American Medical Colleges claims there's a story behind every medical school application. (1) The story of Ann Hansen, DVM, MD, aged 55, a physician in internal medicine at the Boise Veterans Affairs Medical Center in Boise, Idaho, is surely a standout. After ten years of operating a private veterinary clinic, Hansen and her husband, also a veterinarian, decided to take advantage of an opportunity to sell their thriving practice and do something different. For Hansen, that something different was going to medical school.

The decision was a culmination of life experience, says Hansen. "I had a lifelong love of medicine, which I inherited from my father, an old-fashioned physician who specialized in sports injuries and back pain. As a child, I watched as he treated injured weekend athletes in our home, cared for patients, and educated the local ski patrol. He was the kind of physician who stopped to help injured travelers on the highway when we encountered traffic accidents. As a young adult, I worked in his office as a medical assistant."

But after graduating from college in 1980, she enrolled in Tufts University School of Veterinary Medicine, becoming a member of the program's third class. It was a program that emphasized a "one medicine" concept so Hansen attended the same basic science courses as Tufts medical students. During her veterinary residency, which she also completed at Tufts, Hansen developed a strong interest in teaching and subsequently, accepted a one-year faculty position in England. Later, she joined the faculty at Mississippi State University. As a veterinarian, Hansen specialized in equine surgery and athletic injury. "[I] spent many evenings 'talking shop' with my father, who often had helpful suggestions that I applied to my four-legged patients," she says.

When Hansen and her husband opened their own large animal practice in rural Washington State, the new venture was exciting and fun, but it was also a lot of hard work. It was located in a small community, which brought a natural intimacy to the practice, and clients frequently asked Hansen for help with their own medical problems. "I felt remorseful that I was unable to help," she says.

She and her husband had been steadily building their practice, when Hansen's father-in-law became seriously ill. They decided to close the practice temporarily in 2005. At about that same time, an opportunity came along to sell it. "After ten years of constant commitment to the practice, we took some time to reflect," says Hansen. She knew she would be turning 50 just as she began the intense internship portion of her training. But says Hansen, "I still had a passion for academic medicine and teaching and decided that now was the time to follow my father's path." While practicing together day in and day out, her husband often discussed his interest in going to law school. Both decided to seize the opportunity to change careers.

A few people reacted in shock to the decision; some even questioned Hansen's sanity. But her family and close friends were supportive, and she recalls, "One aunt told me that she always thought I would become a physician."

She and her husband liked Louisiana, and after taking the MCAT, Hansen applied to Tulane Medical School in New Orleans. Her application was in process when Hurricane Katrina slammed into the city, forcing the heavily damaged medical school to temporarily relocate. Hansen's interview for admission took place in Houston, the school's temporary headquarters. She was accepted and began her training in August of 2006.

Starting medical school in a city where many of the health-care and training facilities had been under water and shuttered for months required a level of flexibility, but Hansen was up to the challenge. "Post-Katrina New Orleans was an experience," she says. "I was burned out from the veterinary practice, and ready for an adventure. The main concern was to stay safe, as New Orleans was more dangerous at that time." Fortunately, she wasn't alone. "My husband was very supportive and helpful; and I had plenty of time to focus on my safety and living situation, since school was easy for me."

Hansen's veterinary background proved invaluable through medical school and residency. "The biggest challenge of medical or veterinary school is to learn the professional language at an incredibly fast pace and to gain the basic clinical skills," she says. "I was fortunate to already speak the language. After all, we are all mammals." She found the veterinary and medical curricula to be similar, and years of veterinary practice had deepened her understanding of anatomy, physiology, pathology, and pharmacology. Hansen's background and the years that had elapsed since she had taken basic science courses ignited a special enthusiasm for the advances made during the previous 25 years. "In the 1980s, I had many unanswered questions about biochemical mechanisms, and now was fascinated to find out how many of my questions had been answered," says Hansen. "Basic science discoveries, 'dry' course material that my classmates were memorizing for tests, were exciting new horizons for me."

Hansen graduated from medical school in 2010 and recently completed five years of residency. In addition to internal medicine practice, she also conducts research on back pain, primarily for the Boise VA Integrated Spine Care program, and she teaches in the Internal Medicine Residency program affiliated with the University of Washington.

For anyone contemplating medical school after age 50, Dr. Hansen offers some good advice:

– Look at the board exam books and questions offered by the United States Medical Licensing Exam (USMLE) (http://www.usmle.org/) and ask yourself whether you can realistically master this material in the next two years.

– Do some financial research: look at tuition costs, costs for you to complete residency in a likely specialty, and consider your anticipated salary for this specialty—does this make sense?

– Take a realistic look at the time investment in training—four years of medical school, and minimum of three years residency depending on specialty; with no guarantee of getting accepted to medical school or matching in the residency of your choice.

– Anticipate roadblocks: rejection from medical schools, potential age discrimination, need to move to another state, difficulty matching in a residency, and then challenges finding an entry-level job at an older age.

– For school and residency: Eat three squares a day; sleep eight hours a night whenever possible; exercise at least four times a week; take care of yourself! This is a grueling journey that is a marathon, not a sprint.

– If I haven't discouraged you with these real challenges ahead—go for it! People with life experience get so much more out of school; it is a wonderful journey! And never think of the past decades as time lost—this is valuable life experience, which shapes the path ahead.

Those contemplating medical school might be further encouraged by the predicted need for physicians. According to the American Association of Medical Colleges (AAMC), forecasts an increased demand for physicians of up to 17 percent between 2013 and 2025. By 2025, AAMC anticipates the demand for physicians to exceed the supply by a range of 46,000-90,000. (2)

Years of juggling professional and family responsibilities successfully might be the best test of whether or not adding school to the mix is doable. But if there's doubt about taking on another significant chunk of work, prior to committing to a full-time program, enrolling in one class as a test run or studying part-time if it's an option, might be a better way to ease back into academia. I recently met one busy physician who is doing just that: studying for a new undergraduate degree online, taking one course at a time. Not all programs allow part-time study. I inquired about the possibility of studying part-time for the MFA prior to applying to the program, primarily because I wanted to stretch out this special opportunity to learn and hone my craft. Though part-time study wasn't an option, I'm glad I asked so that I wouldn't wonder about it when assignments became more challenging. Programs vary; however, it's certainly worth asking the question up front or consulting with an adviser at your target institution to determine if you can modify the curriculum and develop a plan that is more compatible with goals and needs.

For Stephanie Manriquez, going to school part-time was simply more compatible with her busy work schedule. In 2002, she was teaching and directing the massage therapy program full-time at the community college and running her part-time massage therapy business when she decided to go to work on getting her bachelor's degree. She opted to study part-time in a program that was offered primarily online, saving valuable travel time, and she took advantage of the academic benefits that came with working at the community college, signing up for any course that could transfer and help fulfill requirements for her four-year degree. Still, life was hectic, and her students often asked: "How do you do it all?"

Manriguez's reply was simple. "You have to be organized." Life has always forced her to be organized. "Basically I'm a lazy person. If I can find an easy way to make it happen that's what I do." She developed strategies early on. In her professional cake decorating position, she'd make a list at the end of each day of all the needed to be done the next. She did the same thing at home: who of the six children needed to go where? What had to get done? "There's just a lot of juggling," she says. "There wasn't a lot of time for me."

With more than a full load of work already, Manriquez's approach and philosophy of taking her time in working toward her bachelor's degree made good sense. She typically enrolled in one class at a time, and she took advantage of short, intensive classes that allowed her to snag three credit hours in a weekend. She developed the habit of getting up at 5 a.m. and reading because she would be too tired at the end of the workday. Sometimes she cleaned her house at night because that was the only time left. But she always made room for family. With such a large one, special issues often arose or someone needed help or attention, says Manriquez. But she never lost sight of her broader goals. "I wanted to get the degree, make sure the program was in good shape, and then I wanted to retire." She completed her bachelor's degree in ten years, graduating in 2012. Manriquez has always taken the challenges of juggling so many roles in stride. She's often says, "My life is not vanilla, it's rocky road."

Iris Price of age 76 is a scholar with decades of experience balancing school, family, work, and life. She is about to add to her academic credentials once again—this time with a PhD in Pharmacognosy (botanical medicine). This latest degree is part of a combined master's degree/PhD program at Kingdom College of Natural Health. The dual degree format appealed to Price because of the substantial tuition discount offered to those who enrolled in both. The program's home-study approach also appealed to Price. She uses books and study materials provided by the college, and her research relies on resources found online as well as in texts. Though she has the option of submitting exams and research papers online, she prefers to submit them the way she did when she first started the program: in hard copy. Price completed the master's portion of the program in 2012, and her research projects were accepted, enabling her to continue with her PhD work. The graduation requirements include three theses, and she has already completed the first on the subject of Music Therapy: a drug-free approach to health and healing and the second is titled "Non-Conventional Health Modalities: their use individually and in combination with allopathic medicine."

Though the academic demands at the doctoral level are significant, Price also has a life, and it's a busy one. She stays in touch with grown children and her only granddaughter manages the daily care of Price's assortment of animals--goats, dogs, and chickens. She keeps a schedule of weekly appointments at the hospital for an infusion of rehydration fluids to replace those she is unable to absorb naturally due to longstanding health issues, and she writes a weekly BLOG for an online e-zine. But Price takes it all in stride. She loves to learn, and her deftness at balancing education with jobs, and family, and health challenges is something of a legacy.

Looking back over her path through higher education, Price says, "My advice for those trying to juggle school along with work and family is to decide your priorities. Mine was my little boys, next work, and then furthering my education." Now, as in the past, she doesn't believe in taking on more than she can manage comfortably at one time. "We never know what tomorrow is going to bring, so take it easy and do what you can while still leaving time to 'live.'"

Throughout her many years of studying for various degrees and certifications, Price has remained firm in keeping family her top priority. That was particularly important when her children were young. "I put my sons' needs and wants before my education. I figured that I could always go to school later if I wished, but my sons would need me only for so many years and then they'd be on their own." Price had high standards for mothering. When her sons were about two years of age and were able to hold a pencil, she taught them to read, write, and draw. "We read books all the time and didn't own a TV to clutter their minds," she says. Price describes herself as a strict but loving disciplinarian, so she made sure her sons followed through on their homework and didn't fool around.

The power of time and patient teaching was something Price discovered on her own, back when she was about 12 years old. Every summer, she set up a school for the younger kids in the neighborhood. "I taught them how to read, write, say the alphabet properly, sing, go for nature walks," Price recalls. She was impressed by just how much young children are able to learn if someone had the patience to teach them. It was an idea that stuck with her.

Price has always been interested in learning, and she had hoped to continue her education immediately after high school. The year was 1957, and Price recalls, "I wanted to go to art school when I graduated high school." But her parents were old fashioned and controlling. They allowed her to interview at the Massachusetts Institute of Art, but when she received an acceptance for admission, they refused to let her attend. Instead, they directed her to secretarial school, explaining: a girl needs to learn a skill she can fall back on if her future husband is out of work.

Like so many other young women of the era, Price had no choice but to set aside her own desires and honor her parent's wishes. "I attended Chandler School for Women in Boston and became an unenthusiastic secretary," she says. But as soon as she was old enough to escape at an age considered legal at the time, which was 21, she moved to Florida to live with an aunt and uncle, who believed in education for both boys and girls. They encouraged her to do what she wanted in life. She took a position as a secretary for a manager of a hotel chain in Miami Beach and began seeing some old family friends who had also lived in Massachusetts. Price began dating their nephew who had once lived near her parents. The relationship developed and before long, the couple was married.

The newlyweds moved to the west coast of Florida where Price's husband worked as an engineering assistant, helping to wire the backpack worn by the first man in space. Life got busy quickly. Price gave birth to a son, and the couple adopted a second son 20 months later. Meanwhile, her husband returned to school to study for his bachelor's degree. Later, they relocated so he could continue his education, this time for a master's degree. Meanwhile, Price worked in a childcare center and as a secretary. In order for her husband to study for his PhD, they relocated again, this time, all the way across the country to San Diego. Eventually, there were difficulties. Price began to realize she no longer had much in common with her husband, a man with a fresh PhD in nuclear physics. The couple divorced; the children stayed with Price while her ex-husband took up residence down the street.

That was the early '70s, and the single mom often worked at three jobs. While the children attended school, she worked at a music store during the week, ran a secretarial service from her home, and worked at a tropical fish store during the weekends where she could take her sons along with her. She also battled Crohn's disease, a condition she developed as a child that once landed her in bed for an entire year during her teens. Though her days were full and demanding, Price yearned to return to school.

She changed jobs and began working as a secretary at a water conditioning company. She also enrolled in San Diego Mesa College to study fine and applied art, signing up for one class at a time and riding her motorcycle to campus to save money on gas and parking. Things were chugging along smoothly until the Crohn's disease caused a tumor to develop necessitating major surgery and an extended recovery period. She was forced to defer her studies, though her college advisors invited her to return as soon as she was able.

Several years passed, and when Price was once again able to return to school, she discovered the curriculum had changed. Though advisors allowed her to complete some major courses and shift to selected studies, it was a tough time for her. But she was determined to keep learning and to regain her physical strength as well. After she recovered, her older son bought her a tennis racquet. Her tennis partner also happened to be a runner. Price was inspired. She took up running as well, working her way up to 55 miles a week, a practice she continued for over 31 years. Despite health issues Price says, "I've always been athletic." She combined her athleticism with her love of learning by taking a YMCA course to become certified as a fitness instructor, which gave her another source of income. "I taught fitness classes part-time, in addition to my regular job, from 1981 to 1997," she says. She was also working for the City of San Diego as an information management assistant in the Real Estate Assets Department, a position she didn't retire from until 7 years later. Still working two jobs, she was about to complete her final course at Mesa when news arrived that her mother had passed away. Price missed her final exam. The instructor was sympathetic and in lieu of the exam, allowed her to write an essay on some aspect of local, California history. She researched the history of San Diego, its origins, and the naming of certain areas. The essay earned her an A, allowing her to graduate, and the instructor asked to use her essay in future classes as a model of excellent writing. Price received her Associate's Degree in 1991, but she skipped the graduation ceremony due to the cost.

A few years after graduating Price began looking at what to learn next. "I got curious about online courses and started checking to see what was available at no cost," she says. She found classes focused on landscape and all sorts of short courses online. "I took them just because I like to learn and they were interesting." It's a diversion from real life, she says. Unlike many, Price doesn't watch TV—except for Lawrence Welk reruns on Saturday night. She prefers to learn instead, which gives her a great sense of satisfaction and other benefits. Says Price, "I understand that continually challenging one's brain can, perhaps, stave off dementia."

Eventually, she decided to delve more deeply into design and signed up for an online course offered through the New York School of Interior Design, receiving certification in 1996. Next, she turned to Feng Shui, enrolling in an online program at the Feng Shui Institute of America, obtaining that certificate in 2001. Somewhere in between the two programs, Price's life unfolded in another interesting way. After being single again for 25 years she says, "I married a man whom I met at the bus stop while we were waiting to catch the bus to go to work. He also worked for the City of San Diego, but in a different department than I did. We got married in 1997, about three years after we met."

Her interest in art and decorating remained strong, and she found a landscape design course offered through the Professional Career Development Institute, School of Landscape Design, receiving yet another certificate in 2004. The home study format allowed her to learn in the comfort of her own home. When it came to tests and larger landscape projects, she shipped them directly to the school.

"I'm a visual-kinesthetic person rather an auditory one," she says. She reads fast and thinks fast and likes the home study format. But she admits, there are a few exceptions: specifically, nonacademic courses by Richard Lederer. "There would be no book to compare to listening to him!" says Price. But for academic work, unless an instructor is giving the class information that can't be found in a text, Price prefers to do readings on her own at home and ask questions later. "In a classroom," she says, "the pace is usually set by the slowest learner." She recommends home study for people who like to move at their own pace. Some courses, such as those she took in applied art, require equipment, demonstrations, and shared materials necessitating a classroom. Some students prefer to be in a classroom or feel they benefit from learning in the company of others, says Price. But in addition to being able to move at your own pace, there are other perks to home study. "No traveling to class, no need to be there at a certain time, and at home, one can study in their pajamas . . . and if one is a fast reader, there is no one to slow them down," she says.

While pondering yet another course, her older son suggested she stop fooling around with certificate programs and go get another degree. Price jumped at the challenge. She first looked for home study courses in interior design since art is her first love. When she didn't find any that looked appealing, she searched for courses in natural health and settled on the bachelor's degree program offered at Clayton College of Natural Health. She enrolled in 2005 in the home-study program that included a variety of science courses, such as biology and physiology, and nonconventional health modalities, such as chiropractic, as well as acupuncture, herbology, naturopathy, homeopathy, and nutrition. She managed to juggle school with part-time work at a local gym, providing childcare and front-desk staffing. Price also lived what she was learning—making choices, such as working out everyday, that were in sync with her increasing awareness of natural health and its influence on the human body. Four years later, she completed her Bachelor's Degree in Natural Health, graduating with high honors.

She decided to keep going and had already enrolled in Clayton's master's program when suddenly the school closed. Several colleges reached out to recruit students left without a program, and Price decided the Master's/PhD program at Kingdom College of Natural Health suited her. She chose herbology as her master's subject as she loves herbs and grows them on her farm. Price also had an established knowledge base of herbs and other plants from taking three years of free Saturday morning classes at a local garden nursery, so herbology was a good fit.

Conquering a vast amount of coursework solo is something Price takes in stride. The college offers a forum for posing questions and arranging study buddies, but no one ever responded to her request for a learning companion. Based on the writing style of those posting on to the forum, Price suspects the other members of her student cohort are all younger. "Even the instructors are younger than my sons," she says. "I find that amusing." Most people looking for a study partner are still doing coursework, but for Price, all that's behind her. Now, she is in thesis-writing mode heading toward the home stretch.

Adding college courses to an already busy life might seem impossible. But where there's a will, there's often a willingness to make things work. Taking on responsibilities of school calls for organization and a strong sense of priorities. Support from family can be invaluable, particularly at crunch times, such as during final exams, internships, and residencies. Exploring the possibility of taking classes part-time, getting creative with class format, and being flexible can help expand learning opportunities while still allowing the older student to have a life and manage everyday responsibilities. School + work+ life: it can be done!

---

1. https://www.aamc.org/

2. https://www.aamc.org/download/153160/data/physician_shortages_to_worsen_without_increases_in_residency_tr.pdf

Chapter 6

Encountering Faculty and Fellow Students

"Love all, trust a few, do wrong to none."
– William Shakespeare
(*All's Well That Ends Well,* Act I, Scene 1)

The amount of interaction you have with others in the academic arena often depends heavily on the program and its format. With more opportunities for home study and online learning, these days, it is possible for students to obtain degrees without ever meeting fellow students and professors face-to-face. In other programs, such as professional schools and those involving residencies, more intimate interactions between students as well as with faculty are common, which can present interesting learning opportunities and also pose certain social challenges for older students. However, decades of interacting and working with others can make for an invaluable resource in managing academic relationships as evidenced by these next stories. Of course, a sense of humor always comes in handy as well.

Clarence Nicodemus, PhD, D.O., aged 73, of Monterey, California, believes a physician's role is to help the body heal itself. Board certified in Neuromusculoskeletal Medicine and Osteopathic Manipulative Medicine, Nicodemus takes a "whole person" approach to determining the cause of symptoms and sees the doctor-patient relationship as a partnership that includes education regarding diagnosis and treatment. His practice philosophy is particularly satisfying since for decades, he was limited to helping patients indirectly through his research—until he decided to go to medical school.

Nicodemus was in his late fifties when he entered Michigan State University College of Osteopathic Medicine. He always sat at the front of the class, and often, before things got started, the lecturer would ask: are you a student or a faculty member? He was older than all of the faculty members except one. "I would say without exception, they all had a lot of fun with it," says Nicodemus good-naturedly. Such moments, which many a fifty-something learner might have found unsettling, were tempered by the faculty's respect for the front-row student. Nicodemus already held a PhD and had freshly departed a 30-year career as a biomechanical engineer that included work with NASA and service as director of research for orthopedic spine surgery at the University of Texas Medical Branch at Galveston.

While Nicodemus enjoyed working with astronauts and equipment suggestive of science fiction, he wanted to work more closely with humans. He felt the same yearning in his role as an investigator. His knowledge of the spine, what breaks it and what fixes it, and his work alongside surgeons testing fixators, screws, and nuts and bolts to develop better surgical instruments, often generated questions. "I got to thinking about the people who come into clinic. Many of them were turned away because they weren't surgical prospects," says Nicodemus. He became particularly concerned about these patients who didn't have operable conditions but were still in pain, and he wondered: Where do these people go? What type of specialist cares for them? Back in the mid- to late-90s, their treatment options were typically physical therapy or pain management. "Given my understanding of how the spine works, I got to thinking, why shouldn't I be able to help these folks?" As an engineer, Nicodemus studied and measured people, but he wasn't a healthcare professional; he wasn't licensed to treat patients. Before making any major career decisions, Nicodemus wanted to give himself the opportunity to know if hands-on treatment was something he really liked. He enrolled part-time in a course to become certified in massage therapy. He enjoyed the work, but it gave rise to even more questions about innovative exercises and approaches that might improve various conditions and alleviate pain. Nicodemus began to think about going into osteopathic medicine.

At a meeting of the American Back Society where Nicodemus had presented some research findings, he had the opportunity to talk with the group's president who also happened to be a member of the administrative faculty at MSU's College of Osteopathic Medicine. Nicodemus asked, "Do you take old people such as myself in school?" Given Nicodemus's background, the response was affirmative.

But Nicodemus had yet to broach the subject with his wife. He still recalls the moment. It was a quiet Sunday morning in Galveston, and he and his wife were sitting together reading the newspaper. "I dropped the paper and turned to her and said, 'what would you think if I went to medical school?'"

Her jaw dropped open. "What does that mean exactly?" she asked.

He explained the details, including the necessary move to Michigan. "After we talked through how we would do things and accomplish it, she said, 'yes, let's do it.' Having spousal support was really critical," says Nicodemus. "My wife is a beautiful person inside and out."

Leaving a successful, 30-year career; pulling up roots; and relocating for four years of medical school plus three to four years of residency training prompted a few of his friends to ask: "Are you nuts?" Nicodemus says some told him it was the wrong decision and advised him not to do it.

Nicodemus pressed on. Despite his extensive background in spine research, school administration didn't cut him any slack. He had to study and take the MCAT exam and complete every step of the application process, including the interviews. He was accepted and began coursework in 2000, stepping into a rigorous program that could easily consume in study more hours than each day offered. To get through the first two years, he developed a strategy for studying described in chapter seven. The last two years of the program shifted into the clinical arena, giving students the chance to work with patients. "I just reveled in that," he says.

Age and the human understanding that goes with it gave him an advantage. As his younger peers struggled to develop a sense of empathy, Nicodemus's bounty of life experience enabled him to relate to patients. "It was just a flat-out joy to do that kind of work."

After graduating in 2004 and moving on to internship and residency, the interpersonal aspects of clinical practice continued to be interesting. The typical approach to patient rounds is for less-experienced doctors to gather with an "attending," a seasoned, often older physician, and visit patients as a group to discuss their conditions and treatment plans. Because Nicodemus was often the oldest in the group, patients commonly directed their questions and comments to him, assuming he was the more experienced physician. But most of the attending physicians didn't seem to mind. In fact, being about the same age or older allowed Nicodemus to connect with many of them on a personal level, which didn't always go over well with more senior residents hoping to get noticed. A few got downright irritated; but, says Nicodemus, "Most of the time it was a just a lot of fun."

The intimate interactions between students in an academically intense program such as medical school might create a social environment that magnifies individual differences, including age. In such instances, maturity, once again, can aid in the processing of potentially discomforting social situations.

Dr. Ann Hansen made some interesting observations of the social aspects of attending medical school later in life and offers insights that could be helpful to any older student. "The middle-aged person going back to professional school or residency doesn't have a peer group. You find your social support outside the school microcosm," says Hansen. Though she was going through the same intense academic experiences as her peers, the emotional distance she felt from fellow students was significant. "Professional school in your twenties is a very intense emotional experience with a tight peer group who become friends for life. You do not experience that again. I felt like a fly on the wall, observing but not fully taking part. This allowed me to learn so much about people. It was a lot of fun (like those movies about the news reporter going back to high school on assignment!"

One of Hansen's colleagues, a veterinarian and administrator at a school of veterinary medicine who also attended medical school later in life, found the experience interesting. After two decades of working her busy private veterinary practice, Hansen was humbled even before she began medical school. That background likely aided her in maintaining a graceful restraint in certain situations where it might have been tempting to step forth as an expert. "I often listened dutifully while young interns taught me things I had been doing before they were born. I usually learned something new from their unique perspective. I loved it!"

Hansen makes an interesting point: a student's professional experiences and skills can sometimes exceed those of the teacher, which calls for care in what to share. This interesting situation can occur within many disciplines, particularly in the arts. Fine art, music, dance and theater performance, and the literary arts, present an interesting dichotomy. Because of the product/performance aspect of these disciplines, which plays counterpart to the scholarly dimension, artistic creation and achievement can occur independent of academic certification and credentialing. For instance, an actor who has enjoyed an early career as a performer might later return to school seeking credentials as well as a deeper, academic understanding of the field. In such a scenario, some students might choose to stay entirely below the radar, refraining from revealing their professional background; but in more intimate programs, doing so could prove challenging. Students tend to talk and over time, individual background and experience in the discipline is likely to surface organically.

On the other hand, students with experience in the discipline under study who are inclined to share might anticipate being viewed by faculty as something of a colleague or perhaps a resource able to exchange professional ideas and tips for applying the degree and the knowledge. Some educators might wholeheartedly welcome the infusion of practical, hands-on knowledge from students in class discussions and in fact, might deem the lack of disclosure as an absence of trust. But that is not always the case. Some instructors will feel threatened by a student who exceeds them in professional experience. Of course, there is always safety in silence. On a practical note, prospective students with professional experience, particularly in the discipline they intend to study, would be wise to share that background with an advisor prior to admission to determine if it fulfills credit requirements.

The matter of student history gives rise to broader considerations, particularly in programs that involve ongoing interactions: how much information is too much information? In face-to-face learning forums, professors often ask students to introduce themselves, and those who have arrived with an abundance of life experience but haven't prepared an "elevator speech" might have some fast vetting to do regarding what's important or relevant. The reserved response seems a safe way to go, the humorous one might gain points, but the one the response that can set eyes rolling is the stage-stealer that delivers an oral autobiography. Coming up with a brief personal intro ahead of time can save a great deal of angst. Of course, even with a succinctly delivered introduction, there are no guarantees as to how others will respond.

In Jody Stubler's FNP program, it was customary for students to introduce themselves at the beginning of a course. In one such class, Stubler's mentioned her 22 years of professional nursing experience in the areas of intensive care, emergency room, and school nursing. Immediately following her intro, an ER nurse and fellow student who had inadvertently left her microphone on, responded, "Oh that's not real nursing." Stubler did not get angry or lash out at the student for her insensitive comment, but calmly defended the role of the school nurse. She explained that nurses in schools must be able to function independently without medical backup and distinguish between a stomachache due to not eating breakfast and a case of appendicitis.

Among the 125 enrolled in her family practitioner program, Stubler had one other classmate of comparable age. But she has never been much concerned about relating to younger people. "You can find something to have in common with everyone," she says. Her extensive professional and teaching background set her up to serve as a mentor to some younger classmates. And Stubler often ended up with extra papers to critique for peer review because of her experience and interest in writing. But the help wasn't all one-sided. Younger students mentored her at times too. "We helped each other," she says. With collaborative projects, everyone took a section and student age made no difference. In some instances, age gave her an edge. "I think being older helped me keep things in perspective," she says. When people are upset and overwhelmed by the workload, she often pointed out the solidarity of their circumstances and played out a worst-case scenario to help diffuse tension.

Stubler had an unfortunate experience with one faculty member who urged her to withdraw from the program. The situation developed after Stubler scored low on an early exam then submitted a paper that the instructor critiqued harshly and graded as a C, claiming certain sections were missing. "I knew it was a good paper," Stubler says. As a teacher, she knew the importance of following the rubric to the letter; and she had done so. The grade was also inconsistent with Stubler's track record. In undergraduate and graduate school she had never received lower than an A on papers. The instructor called her aside and explained she wasn't doing well, and urged her to withdraw. Stubler sought guidance and her advisor recommended she stand firm. In response to the grade, Stubler went over the entire paper highlighting the content and sections the instructor claimed were missing. "I had to petition four times before she gave me the points back," she says. In the end, Stubler successfully defended her paper and got her A.

Meanwhile Stubler learned that the other student near her age had received similar treatment but also stayed in the program. It made for a rough semester for Stubler, but she didn't crumble. What's more, she didn't allow it to taint her overall positive experience in the program. "I evaluated my own feelings and thought thank goodness I am older because I can see it for what its worth and shrug it off." Both Stubler and her classmate finished the program with honors. The instructor is no longer working at the institution.

In programs that emphasize artistic expression, students often come to know one another more personally as a natural outflow of the coursework. Showing up for the first residency of my MFA felt like going off to summer camp for the first time. I hadn't met any of my fellow students, except through online homework assignments. At our first residency, we were scheduled not only to meet each other but also to live and learn together for ten days and nights. I turned out to be the oldest, but I was not the only student over 50. As we settled into the program and focused on our writing, I was pleased to discover that the age differences among my peers seemed to melt away. It didn't matter so much where we were in life; we were united by a common goal: we all wanted to become better writers.

The drive and passion for creative, artistic expression sometimes seems to transcend age. One of our poetry exercises involved teams of two writers, each drafting part of a sonnet from a contrasting perspective of the subject, and doing so without discussion or review of the other team member's work. The division of teams was based entirely on seating. I was teamed with one of the younger students sitting next to me—an extraordinarily talented poet. We made a quick decision: he would write the first eight lines; I would write the final seven lines. Then we went off alone to write for a brief, never-long-enough period of time. Neither of us knew how the other had handled the subject, until we read the final product, the full sonnet, aloud to the class. I was astonished to discover how well the two pieces meshed into a single cohesive piece. I wondered if our age difference didn't enhance the turning point of the sonnet and thus, enrich the entire piece. The whole thing felt like a magic trick, and the exercise caused me to wonder if the arts might be an ideal arena for intergenerational collaboration.

Relationships formed in higher education hold the potential to turn into creative partnerships, business associations, and even lifelong friendships. But of course, as in any arena, wherever two or more people are gathered, there is opportunity for misunderstanding. One of the biggest risks of such situations is that they can become distractions from work and study. However, the student with five decades or more of accumulated life experience more than likely has a level of hardiness and determination to rise above awkward moments and to manage any potential conflicts. Having a supportive individual or network outside the classroom can also be invaluable to regaining the necessary focus to carry on. And those working in the arts might well find that social awkwardness, painful interpersonal exchanges, and even invisibility can become raw material and inspiration for creative expression. For others, it's another layer of life experience that might just make you stronger.

Chapter 7

Making the Program Your Own

"This above all—to thine own self be true."
– William Shakespeare
(*The Tragedy of Hamlet, Prince of Denmark,* Act I, Scene 3)

For Dr. Clarence Nicodemus, prioritizing areas of study proved invaluable during the first two years of medical school, which is the intense academic segment that is loaded with sciences, including biochemistry, anatomy, pharmacology, and pathophysiology. The first semester was particularly difficult, says Nicodemus. "It was a challenge for me to get back into the mindset of studying. I was really hard-pressed to keep up."

That first semester taught him an important lesson: he learned how he needed to learn. He came up with an approach that differed from the way he learned earlier in life. "When I was younger I could read the text, I could retain the material. I could take the exam," he says. "Here, much of it was memorization, so I had to sort of develop a way of learning that enabled me to retain the material." Time was a major issue; there wasn't enough of it to study everything. "I had to really analyze the course material and decide what was the important part." Once he got accustomed to the flow of a course and discerned what the instructor emphasized as important, he focused his attention on those specific areas and took hits on the parts he wasn't able to study.

If you're older, there are certain facts you can't deny, says Nicodemus. For one, you don't learn the same way you did when you were younger, so just accept that fact. "Take a course or two to learn how you learn. You can do anything you want to do when you put your mind to it, but you have to accept the fact that you have to do it differently than you did when you were younger." You study differently and approach it differently, but there are compensating factors. Nicodemus says life experience and maturity enable you to make judgments about the study material. At a younger age, you don't have the same background to distinguish the critical material from that which is less important. With 60 years of life experience, you're better prepared to make decisions and focus your study efforts on what you feel is most important, Nicodemus says. "You make the education yours. It's a whole different education concept than what it was when you were a kid. You learn what you want to learn. At this point, you don't care about the grades." Passing, of course, is important, but it's not necessary to be at the top of the class. At the end of the first two grueling years of medical school's purely academic work, Nicodemus fell somewhere in the middle of the pack for class rankings. "I wasn't on the top like I used to be. But I wasn't on the bottom either, he says. The next two years of clinical experiences--participating in externships and working with patients--were an entirely different story. Performing clinical procedures and working with patients, Nicodemus excelled.

Some academic programs allow flexibility enabling students to do a little exploring and tweaking to shape the coursework to meet individual interests and goals. In the Spring of 2016, *Cathy, aged 54, of Chagrin Falls, Ohio, will graduate with a Master's Degree in Educational Psychology from Kent State University, a degree that will be invaluable to the program she has developed to help young adults make informed and intentional choices about their lives. She remembers the time before she decided to return to school. "I was feeling sad…I felt like I hadn't achieved what I wanted to achieve." There had been plenty of jobs and moves, and she loved being a mother of three, but there was the ever-present thought in back of her mind that she hadn't really applied her gifts, talents, and skills to a career. Cathy had done tons of volunteer work, earned a certificate in mediation, and she had always challenged herself to learn new things. But she wasn't entirely satisfied; she wasn't where she wanted to be.

Cathy attended college immediately after high school, not really knowing exactly what she wanted to do. She got a degree in finance in 1984 and married at age 23. She worked in banking for many years and hated it. She says, "It was just not a great fit for me." But she kept at it, working until she was 30, and then she started a family. She had the desire to go back to school, but with three children and a husband who traveled frequently, she hesitated. "I didn't think I had the time. I didn't think I had the support. I didn't think I could pull it off." She waited for the time to be right.

Later, during a parents' weekend party at her son's college, Cathy happened to get into a conversation with another mom. "She told me she had gone back to school for counseling at about the same age that I was right then," says Cathy. "I was so interested in what she had done, and she said, 'you could do that.'" If I hadn't met her, I don't know that I would have made the decision to return to school, says Cathy. "It truly made a difference to me, and I don't even remember her name."

When her youngest reached the seventh grade, her middle child was able to drive, and Cathy was approaching 50, she decided it was time to give graduate school a try. It was kind of my fiftieth birthday present to myself, she says.

She was accepted into Kent State University, about a 45-minute drive from home. Her program did not require her to take the GRE because of her undergraduate GPA, and it allowed her to study part time, so Cathy planned to take one or two classes per semester. At first, she says, "I wasn't sure exactly what I wanted to study. She knew from all her volunteer work, particularly in her children's school, that she was interested in working with young adults to help them choose a career. She had long struggled with her own career choices and thought she might be able to help others facing similar challenges. She figured the counseling program was a good place to start. When Cathy initially crunched the numbers on how long it might take to accumulate enough credits to graduate, she came up with a total of six years to finish, which is the limit for grad school at Kent University. She shared her concern with a friend: "I don't know, does this make any sense? I'll be 55 when I graduate."

Her friend replied, "Well, you'll be 55 anyway, you might as well be 55 and have the degree."

Fortunately, Cathy had the chance to serve on the counselor's advisory committee at her child's school, which allowed her to work closely with school counselors and observe first hand the real nature of their work. It turned out she was really interested in focusing on a segment of those responsibilities, not everything the role demanded. That experience reinforced for Cathy her own belief in the importance of getting out of the academic setting to see how things actually work. She shifted away from the counseling program and decided to take some classes in higher education, student development, and service learning, which allowed her to do an internship in the career center of a local college. She also co-taught a class at Kent for college freshman focused on career navigation. "I really learned a lot about college student development and what's going on with them in those years." Still, the fit wasn't entirely right. "There were things I liked and things I didn't like," says Cathy. Plus, she discovered that higher education was designed as a cohort program with very specific course requirements to be completed during a two-year period. "There was very little flexibility," she says. Required were classes such as Business Law that Cathy knew she wouldn't use, and at her age, she didn't have the patience for classes that weren't relevant to what she wanted to do.

She began to look more seriously at educational psychology because of its flexibility and opportunities to customize her studies. Since all of her coursework had taken place within the same college of the university, making the transition was easy. "Ed Psych was perfect for designing a program that I could implement," says Cathy. In order to create such a program she really needed to understand better how individuals learn and how to motivate people. The shift to educational psychology allowed her to take a series of classes in human motivation and a course in adolescent development, which gave her insights as to young adults' readiness to make decisions. Cathy's advisor allowed her to replace classes that where similar to what she had taken in the past with ones that were relevant to her interests. "I learned a lot about the brain and neuroscience," says Cathy. "I was just so lucky that I had the flexibility . . . and was able to put together a collection of classes that's really appropriate for what I wanted to do." Because Cathy switched from counseling to educational psychology, which required fewer credits for graduation, the time she took trying classes in different areas of emphasis did not extend her time in graduate school, and she's finishing up within five years. She also took advantage of the option to take more classes in lieu of writing a thesis.

The academic flexibility allowed Cathy, to a great degree, to make the program her own. Of course, not everyone can understand the desire for this level of academic commitment later in life. Periodically, people wondered about Cathy's plans for the new degree, asking: What are you going to do with that? "To me, that's a put down," says Cathy. It suggests my choice is somehow a waste of time. But Cathy has wasted no time putting her education to good use—even before graduating. About two-and-a-half years ago, mid-way through her studies, she developed a program to help young adults figure out what they want to do with their lives. Over the course of five sessions, Cathy works one-on-one with high school juniors and seniors, and college students. She starts by helping them clarify their identity through self-reflection and writing. The next step is exploring career options that might be a good match for who they are, with the idea that a good fit will likely prove more satisfying and lead to greater success. Then she helps create an action plan with some short term goals that help them continue to gather information and ultimately, make good decisions. Cathy emphasizes the gathering of information part of the program. You can't really make a good decision until you have more information. You have these pre-conceived notions about what you think things are like, but you have to go and test it, she says. "I don't tell them what to do at any point in time," says Cathy. "I never do that. I really facilitate their self-discovery and exploration and then help to motivate them to take the next step to do the things they need to do to reach the goals that they want."

Cathy understands the importance of this kind of work on a deeply personal level. "What I do is meaningful to me because I want to prevent other people from making the mistakes that I made," she says. When she was younger, she didn't do any career planning and suffered the consequences. "I just kind of floated through and didn't give my major much thought. I didn't give my career choice much thought. I just sort of let things happen to me." When she accepted a job, she says, "It was not an educated decision, and so I feel like I wasted a lot of time and energy, and it's demoralizing when you put yourself in a situation where you're not a good fit." She often dismissed her feelings as well. "I tend to error on the side of logic," she says. I would come up with a plan without really taking my feelings into account, pushing them aside as if they weren't really important. "That's wrong because you have to live with what you've chosen," she says.

Cathy's program is designed to help young people develop a decision-making process that they can use over and over in their lives. "I've really tried to advocate for kids to get as much information as they can—do your reading, do your research but also talk to people, get out and try things, get the internships, do the jobs, do the volunteer experiences, get as much information as you can but then make sure you're thinking about how you feel too, and working that into the equation," she says. When making important decisions about career, says Cathy, you want to use your reasoning powers to look at information objectively, but then you also want to ask yourself how you feel about it. You want to take both aspects into account.

Cathy also doles out plenty of encouragement, which she believes is especially important when working with a young population. They might have what seems like a crazy goal. She encourages them to get as much information as possible and reflect again on their goals to determine if adjustment is warranted.

Cathy is pleased with her decision to return to school. In addition to the mom she met that parents' weekend who encouraged her to go back to school, Cathy also credits a fourth-grader whose little comment helped her reach the tipping point. The young girl told her, "Your 'want' has to be bigger than your 'can't.'"

It has been downright rejuvenating to pursue her academic interests at this point in her life. "I love to learn," says Cathy. "I am so energized. I get so excited. I love it."

---

* Requests reference to her first name only.

Chapter 8
Tackling Technology

"Nothing can be loved or hated unless it is first understood."
                                    – Leonardo da Vinci

Take Blackboard, Canvas, and Moodle, toss in some Skype, Google Chat, Slack Channel, add a few Webinars, sprinkle in a bit of Wordpress, add bits of social media such as Facebook, Twitter, LinkedIn, Instagram, Pinterest, etc., etc., and suddenly the cumulative load of technology feels overwhelming. Collectively, these platforms and media pulls also make you wonder: how do we ever get anything done away from our computers?

If the last time you showed up for a class exam was with a Blue Book and a trusty Number 2 pencil, you might want to brush up on your computer skills and learn a few programs before heading back to school. The technical aspects of higher education coursework can be particularly intimidating, if not downright terrifying. But fear not! Resources are in abundance to help fill the knowledge gap and build skills. Technical knowledge builds on itself and mastering one of these programs often makes tackling the others a little easier.

Technology is not only a way of daily life, it is also the means to accomplish most processes associated with school, from registering for classes and testing, to participating in online discussions and submitting assignments, theses, and dissertations. Most colleges and universities offer training and support, sometimes one-on-one, for tech-based programs and software, and many local libraries and community centers offer instructional programs to help master academic technologies. This tangential aspect of returning to school not only builds technical skills for life, it helps build confidence and might well inspire an entirely new idea, such as launching a blog or starting an online business.

Learning and mastering more technology is, in my opinion, well worth the struggle.

Linda Webb vividly recalls one of her first college courses. Each member of the class sat down in front of a computer to begin working. The professor strolled about the classroom but came to a stop beside Webb who hadn't made a move. "We're ready to start," the professor said.

Webb responded, "I don't know how to turn it on." The instructor directed her to take a different computer class before enrolling in the one she had signed on for. Webb laughed at herself at the time, but inside, her feelings were hurt. Still, she realized she would be lost staying in the more advanced class trying to struggle through. The instructor was right. Webb made her way to the computer skills lab located in the college library. Every minute she wasn't in class she was in the lab learning more about the computer.

When her skills had improved sufficiently, Webb returned to the more advanced class once again. The instructor welcomed her back, revealing then that she'd noticed a distinct determination about Webb and a willingness to learn. "I had some very patient, understanding teachers who stuck with me," says Webb.

Given the speed at which technology changes, it's easy to fall behind, particularly after years of working in a field that isn't heavily dependent upon computer systems. Dr. Ann Hansen says, "The biggest challenge for me, from the first day of medical school, through the residency, and even today—is the computer." As an undergraduate, she remembers seeing the one computer on campus that filled a small room with its mysterious system of electronics. Hansen finished her undergraduate degree never having to touch a computer. She took an Introduction to Programming course in veterinary school, but when she began practicing she had secretaries to manage computer tasks. Though she eventually learned a little word processing and gained a glimpse of the Internet world, it wasn't enough for medical school. "I scrambled to improve my computer skills," says Hansen. "I struggled with this through training, and still struggle…"

Using technology to manage daily life and communications can provide a skill base to operate from in learning more complex programs encountered in Higher Ed. But some coursework demands skills that will steepen the learning curve dramatically.

When Cathy began working on her master's degree, her biggest initial challenge was technology. "Back when I was in college, we didn't have personal computers . . . I went to Penn State undergrad, and my class was the first not to have these punch cards for computer science." While Cathy uses electronic devices for email, word processing, and other needs, she doesn't have a lot of interest in technology. Her master's program pushed her to learn more, particularly the class focused on technology and learning.

"I had to create instructional videos and do all this tech stuff, so I really had to learn a lot about that, and when I did my internship, it was very obvious how far behind I was. . . . That was kind of a rude awakening but I got through it," says Cathy. She was required to take one course online because the focus of the class was online learning and studying the various instructional materials and technology needed to support this approach. Though Cathy says this form of learning has its place, depending on a person's situation, she prefers attending classes in person.

"I like discussions . . . I like the classroom experience. I like to talk to people," she says. She found the online participation and homework to be more work than going to classes for a couple of reasons. In trying to create an online community and urging students to feel connected, there is a system for keeping track of the number of times individuals respond to the posts of others. Cathy says it's not enough to simply put forth an opinion; it needs to be a thoughtful, educated comment, preferably one that includes a citation. Though online learning isn't her favorite forum, Cathy admits, "I learned a ton."

She believes it took her longer to master these skills than it did for some of the younger students in the program. During her internship, she was able to do much of the learning on the job, which allowed her to work with others to learn and troubleshoot.

"The other thing," says Cathy, "You can YouTube anything!" She spent hours at the computer practicing. "I really kind of overdo everything," she says. "That's just who I am. She kept at it until she had mastered the skills she needed. "It really felt good. It's kind of empowering."

Most people returning to school after a long academic gap expect to expand their technology skills, but few go from beginner to guru. Stephanie Manriquez got her first computer back in 1997, a year before she entered community college to study massage therapy. At first, she was constantly calling her oldest son, the computer expert of the family, to ask questions. Gradually, she began learning more and more on her own, and she took some classes to help build her skills. But things have changed. During the last six or seven years, she has become the technology go-to person in the family. Her son is blown away by the fact she has surpassed him in technical skills. She played a similar role before retiring as director of COCC's massage therapy program. Her program was the first on campus to start using ipads. Since the campus lacked the technical support for the devices, Manriquez's program served as a campus resource for other departments seeking to expand technology.

I expected to push beyond my technical comfort zone when I returned to school. For me it was a positive as I have a tendency to work around using technology if I can find a detour. We began the MFA program by posting assignments on Blackboard, which I had never used in my undergraduate coursework, but it was relatively straightforward and learning a new form of electronic communication was a confidence-builder. Technically, it didn't seem any more difficult than copying and pasting text from a Word document into an email. The anxiety that prompted extra proofing and hesitation over clicking the "Post" button was due to the nature of the recipients—a class of students and faculty nearly all of whom I had never met. I was both relieved and impressed by the polite responses, comments, and e-introductions that began to appear every time I visited Blackboard. As we became better acquainted (electronically), I got a little more comfortable posting my work and started to imagine the people associated with the comments and writing styles, and their frequency and manner of communicating and responsiveness to other students. In a program focused on writing, this made for an interesting electronic introduction and added to the anticipation of residency a couple of months later when we could finally meet the people who went with the prose. It was like going on a collective blind date.

Though there were some glitches in the system now and then and at times, the university shut the entire program down for repairs, Blackboard proved easy to use. Just as I started to take a little pride in the ease and speed of my clicking, cutting, pasting, and posting, an announcement came via email: a thing called Canvas was replacing my new friend, Blackboard.

By that time, I was too busy with coursework and thesis to learn any more about this new system than what was absolutely necessary to post assignments by deadline, which was ominously calculated to the final hour assignments were due. My distrust of the new program led me to submit assignments even earlier than my usual habit of beating deadlines. Canvas must have sensed my reluctance to fully embrace it and had its revenge when I assumed responsibility for submitting one of my class's group projects. It was up to me to make deadline for the entire group, so I allowed plenty of time for technical glitches, power outages, and server failures. I logged in, attached the document, and clicked submit. Canvas responded immediately to the assignment with a single word: "LATE." My heart pounded. I double-checked the date, the time, even the time zone. It was hours before the deadline. We were NOT late. Canvas was wrong! But I was responsible for my entire cohort's assignment. I hadn't goofed; there was some sort of glitch in the technology. I emailed the faculty member, explained what had happened, asked for advice and copied all the members of my class so everyone was aware of what had happened. The instructor responded that the assignment had been received and we were all fine. Canvas and I, however, have lingering trust issues.

The beauty of expanding technical skills within a university system is having access to support. Computer-related problems can be frustrating and time-consuming. On a couple of occasions, I had difficulty with a program and formatting issues, and called the university computer help desk. These patient, technical geniuses who staff such offices are Higher Ed's unsung heroes, calmly step-by-stepping people out of their technical jams.

Another matter related to use of technology that deserves serious consideration is the nature and quality of electronic communication—in short, electronic etiquette. Widespread use of on-line and distance-learning formats means possibly never meeting face-to-face with other members of the class, even the instructor. While communicating without video capability, does remove all the visible signs of aging, it also presents a special opportunity for misstep and miscommunication. Without the accompaniments of facial expressions and body language to help our words, those on the receiving end of such messaging form an impression based on prose alone. Etiquette related to online communications, particularly email, matters and many colleges and universities provide guidelines that can keep students from stumbling. The University of Wisconsin is one example of an institution that posts online its policies and guide for best practices (http://cits.uwex.uwc.edu/policies). The University of Minnesota has put together a guide specific to keeping emails professional (http://umcf.umn.edu/resources/emailguide.php). A good overarching principle to keep in mind: never consider emails to be private. They are easily forwarded and may be monitored by university administrators.

Chapter 9

Papers, Tests, Grades, and Distinction

"Some are born great, some achieve greatness,
and some have greatness thrust upon 'em."
– William Shakespeare
(*Twelfth Night*, Act II, Scene 5)

Grades can be a touchy subject for students of any age. History and tradition, parental influences, past achievements and disappointments, etc. Any of these factors alone or in combination can make for a complex relationship with test grades, grade point averages, and other measures of academic success and distinction. If you grew up with parents who doled out financial rewards for good grades and grounded you for not-so-great ones, the judgment of others might be inextricably tied to academic achievement. Perhaps you've tried to change that pattern with your own children, emphasizing learning over getting a high grade. Though time and life experience might have eased the tension around these traditional forms of academic evaluation, the ghost of grades can continue to haunt us despite all rational attempts to disempower it.

Some programs are set up as pass/fail, but many take a more traditional approach of awarding grades but vary widely as to process of achieving them. Online courses often mean online tests, so achieving a level of comfort with technology before test time is important to success. Some programs might require a rigorous combination of written tests and observational evaluation of skills through student demonstration, while others allow students to grade themselves. Graduate level programs often require oral exams, theses, or dissertations.

For sure, being graded again after decades of functioning outside the academic environment can come as a bit of a shock. Stephanie Manriquez had to readjust her thinking about grades when she returned to school. "In the beginning . . . I didn't understand the seriousness of classes, and I got lackadaisical on one of them and didn't get all of the work done." She apologized to the instructor and pledged to do better following through on the details of assignments the next time, but the poor grade held. "I paid attention after that," says Manriquez.

Abandoning a lifelong drive to achieve at the highest level can be difficult, if not impossible. And the perception that the older student is the underdog can sometimes serve to further fuel the drive to greater heights of achievement.

When Jody Stubler was studying for her master's degree, her husband and family tried to take the pressure off by saying, "It's okay to get a B." Stubler agreed, sort of. She wanted to graduate with a 4.0. "I know if I just work a little harder, I can get an A, and I want to see if I can do it," she would tell herself. She accomplished her goal, which ultimately gave her the confidence she needed to apply to a top family nurse practitioner program.

The FNP program was intense. Once or twice a year, Stubler flew to Georgetown for a week of examination and evaluation. It took a score of 84 or above to pass each class. The courses were heavy with content, and the arduous testing process was often cumulative and aimed to evaluate not only student knowledge but also the ability to apply it in a clinical setting. "My first semester was incredibly hard," Stubler recalls. "We had advanced pathophysiology and advanced pharmacology. I think I cried everyday, wondering: what have I done? Stubler had underestimated the amount of information she'd be required to learn in one semester, and the exams were some of the hardest she had ever taken in her life. For the first month or so, she struggled and had to remind herself daily of why she had wanted to return to school at this phase of her life: "you're doing this for the children, you're doing this for your grandchildren," she says. Finally, Stubler got downright harsh with herself: "Enough!" she said, "You're doing this, so stop your moaning and groaning and get to work."

When already feeling overwhelmed with coursework and studying, an insensitive comment can shake your faith, but in Jody Stubler's case, such a remark made her all the more determined. The friend reminded her that she was 60 years old and was competing with younger minds, with students in their 20s and 30s. "Oh my goodness!" Stubler says. "That's all you had to say to me, and I thought, I'm going to show you!" She got through that tough first semester. The second semester required Advanced Assessments, another difficult course. At the end of 12 weeks, students had to show what they had learned by conducting a head-to-toe assessment on a patient while being observed and evaluated by two instructors as well as the patient. Only one student received a score of 100 percent on the assessment and the final exam—that student was Stubler. After receiving the news that she had aced the assessment, she called her friend to share the news. She says, "Guess this sixty-year-old mind isn't that old after all!"

In a program that incorporates online testing, mastering technical skills beforehand is critical; otherwise, the test might turn into a measure of technological mastery than knowledge of course content. Karen Love completed the entire program for her Master's Degree in Gerontology online, including timed tests. She credits her daughter with helping her to master some of the more challenging technical issues beforehand. Says Love, "She was a big help to me. She said 'mama just calm down. You're going to be okay.' She kind of hung over my shoulder ... and showed me some short cuts." In terms of final requirements, USC did things a bit differently, Love says. She was required to write papers for at least three different 500-level courses. For one of her papers, she paired up with a cyber-buddy in Massachusetts. "We did an in-depth comparison study in Michigan and Massachusetts on the Green House Concept founded by geriatrician Bill Thomas, cofounder of the Eden Alternative (http://www.edenalt.org/). She wrote a second paper on transforming communities and the third related to the LGBT community.

Love admits that getting through the final requirements without the benefit of face-to-face time with a professor took skill. As for the beliefs that helped her reach the finish line, Love says, "Being at peace with your work, knowing that you've done your best, and that your work will take you places...." Her advice for others: never doubt yourself, your talent, or your abilities because you're over age 60. But, says Love, "Don't be afraid to ask for help. That's very important."

Papers such as theses and dissertations mean living with a subject for an extended period of time. Submitting those documents for credit or grading typically demands a different kind of nuts and bolts handling.

Iris Price found the biggest challenge to thesis writing to be following the precise format and required writing style. The three theses she is writing to fulfill her PhD requirements have given her a few insights as to achieving success. Her simple advice: "Read the instructions before starting to write! Then, read them again!" In the course of gathering information, note the sources. And if the subject is not pre-assigned, Price says, select a topic that interests you. Read and re-read your written work, and do some work on it every day – once you start skipping days, it's easy to fall behind.

For those who have a history of high achievement, self-imposed pressure to achieve comparable grades and cumulative grade point averages can be significant. But if the goal of returning to school is purely to learn the material, grades can become a distraction, and finding a way to de-emphasize the grading aspect of the program can be invaluable to the learning process.

When Dr. Nicodemus entered medical school, he developed a refreshing take on grades within the broader context of learning. Rather than getting hung up on grades and class rankings, he developed a personal plan for study (described in chapter seven) that allowed him to stay focused on the learning.

Two of my favorite features of the low-residency MFA

program design were: the lack of tests and assigning our own grades. I'll admit, or perhaps I should confess, I gave myself A's. I felt that I had honestly earned them. But I also felt my fellow students, all enthusiastic, hard-working writers, had earned A's as well. And I included this point as an additional comment on my self-grading forms.

Though the MFA was a pass/no pass program, it did require both a thesis and an oral exam. The thesis was a creative body of work, in my case, a substantial portion of a young adult novel. Most of the challenges related to thesis submission were related to formatting and technical issues, as I described in the previous chapter. I was more anxious about the oral exam portion of the requirement, which meant being the center of attention amid a group of four faculty members. In addition, prior to the oral exam, they were expected to read my thesis, which ran about a hundred pages. I worried they already had too much to do, and half of the faculty were men, and surely they would be bored reading a portion of a YA novel about a young girl growing up in the 1960s. My anxious tendency was to thank the committee members repeatedly, but that still seemed insufficient. Much to my surprise, the exam went smoothly; ultimately, it became an hour of opportunity to discuss and respond to questions about my work.

At the end of the exam session, I was asked to wait outside the meeting room while my committee of four faculty members, half of whom Skyped in for the session, deliberated. It took less than five minutes. When they called me back inside, my mentor enthusiastically announced, "Congratulations! You passed!"

I smiled unenthusiastically, and quietly said, "Thank you." But questions filled my brain. Passed? Is that all? No distinction? Just a 'pass'? I knew I should be happy, but all I could think of: I hadn't passed; I had passed without distinction. And that felt like failure. I tried not to show my disappointment. But as I walked out of the room and into the rest of the day, it weighed on my mind. I had done all the work, made all the deadlines, participated fully in all the residencies. To be entirely honest, I believed my entire student cohort was so talented and special, everyone deserved distinction! We were the first class of the program—the guinea pigs. We were flexible, spirited, supportive; in my opinion, we all deserved distinction.

I'll admit, it took a little time and some processing, but eventually, I came around to cataloguing all that I hadn't done. I hadn't participated in the program's extra offerings and volunteer opportunities. Instead, I had chosen to focus entirely on the coursework and my writing while managing life responsibilities at the same level as before entering the program. The latter detail was particularly important to me. Although I had never been informed of the criteria for achieving distinction in the program, I had never taken the responsibility to ask either. But it was a little late for those particular kinds of questions.

At first, I considered talking to my mentor then decided against it. To do so would have felt awkward, childish, and whiny, as if I was asking, "Why doesn't anyone think I'm special?" But I was curious and began wondering if I had performed badly during the oral exam, but because I was so nervous I hadn't realized it. We had houseguests in the days immediately preceding the oral exam, right up until the hours before the exam. Perhaps I had been too distracted. As I drafted final emails of thanks to each member of my exam committee, I considered asking one of the faculty members I had only communicated with by email and never actually met. He was not affiliated with the MFA program, but rather was a professor of environmental ethics who had Skyped in for the exam to serve as a Graduate Council Representative, a mandatory member of the committee who assures compliance with university policies and procedures. I was particularly grateful for his time and effort as part of his role involved reading 100 pages of a thesis that had nothing to do with his area of expertise. His questions during the exam had been particularly thoughtful, and it seemed he had a lot of experience participating in oral exams. I decided to take a risk in my thank-you email and opened up about the outcome of the exam. I admitted to being old fashioned about grades and troubled that I had merely passed and was concerned I had performed badly during the exam. I assured him I could take constructive criticism, and welcomed any and all feedback on what I should have done better.

He responded with an email, explaining that pass/no pass were the only two grading options for the graduate school. The "with distinction" seemed specific to the program, and at the end of the day, these things are more judgments than they are measurements. He went on to say my defense was quite good and that I was very poised and answered questions with as much clarity as the questions themselves called for. He noticed a clear sense that I was speaking more as a colleague than a student. What he especially appreciated were my moral instincts with regard to the cautious treatment of the characters in my novel and resistance to using shock, adding: "That speaks volumes for you as both a writer and as a person - we need a bit more Gandhi in a world that's become so Trump!" I replied with enormous thanks.

That was all the distinction I needed. I passed. I graduated. I could move on to the rest of my life.

Chapter 10

Making an Impact, Deciding What's Next

"Were there none who were discontented with what they have, the world would never reach anything better."
                                        – Florence Nightingale

The impact of returning to school later in life can make a significant difference not only in our own lives, but also in the lives of others by: providing an innovative approach to healthcare, helping young people make good life choices, developing new programs, and assisting special education students in believing in themselves. When I asked those who shared their stories what they have planned next, I wasn't surprised to discover there was no hint of idleness. Here are some of the ways these scholars are making a difference and continuing to reach new heights of achievement.

For Jody Stubler, the Hope Family Medical Center is a dream come true. When the clinic launched two years ago, it was only Stubler and her office manager, Karen Duarte, handling daily operations. Stubler saw every patient who came through the door, which usually ran around eight per day. Her plans to grow the staff slowly to increase patient capacity while still keeping the amount of time spent with patients and the quality of care high have paid off. Nearly two years later, Stubler says, "We have grown by leaps and bounds and are going strong." The Center is now buzzing with two part-time medical assistants, two receptionists, two billers and coders, as well as volunteers and students. Stubler is pleased. "It's working. I love what I'm doing." Her experience in teaching has come in handy as the Center provides training opportunities for students in nursing and other health professions. Shortly after opening, the Hope Center added a charitable arm, establishing a foundation to assist patients who need endoscopy, MRIs, or surgery but are unable to pay. Two fundraisers to benefit the foundation took place, one in the fall of 2015 and another in February 2016. The funds have helped a patient needing cataract surgery and have provided assistance patients needing medications, CT scans, x-rays, and consultations with specialists and other procedures the clinic is unable to offer.

"I went through an amazing journey," Stubler says. Occasionally people ask if she would do it all over again, and she responds with enthusiasm: "In a heartbeat!" I jumped through a million hoops to graduate with honors from a top program and that gave me the confidence to jump through a million more to set up my own clinic, she says. "How often they say after 60 your ability to learn goes down. Well that's bogus. And I'm proof of that." I graduated less than two years ago, and "Here I am 64 years old, and I'm running my own business." You can learn anything you want to learn, do anything you want to do if you put your mind to it.

For the past nine years, Dr. Clarence Nicodemus has been treating patients through a private practice in Monterrey, California (http://www.montereyclinic.com/home.htm), with the help of wife, Grace, the author of E*ating With Grace: Learning to Feed Your Body and Nourish Your Life*, who provided business oversight and worked with patients to alleviate factors such as stress and weight control that can exacerbate pain and influence health. Nicodemus, known for employing nonsurgical approaches based on human anatomy and basic physics and engineering principles, says, "You can do a lot of things short of slicing people up." He uses caution when prescribing drugs and administering injections, and though he does use injections for pain relief, he feels it's the work on the table, often on a weekly basis and reinforced with exercises that makes the difference. Nicodemus believes the body knows where it wants to go. You just have to help it along.

"I actually love working with patients and solving problems," says Nicodemus. All he has learned through clinical practice these past eight years has enabled him to make slight modifications in treating patients. It also generated more questions that remain unanswered in existing literature—questions that fueled a deep desire to undertake new areas of scientific research. Last fall at the age of 74, Nicodemus made a major career move that will give him the opportunity to discover answers to some of these lingering clinical questions. He accepted a faculty position at Michigan State University College of Osteopathic Medicine where he attended medical school. In his new role as Clinical Director of Biomechanics Research, Nicodemus is undertaking the kind of research that will have a direct impact on patient care and treatment.

In addition to conducting back pain research and teaching internal medicine residents, Dr. Ann Hansen's role in general internal medicine involves both outpatient and inpatient care. "I take care of sick veterans and, by extension, their families. This is truly a privilege," says Hansen. Her plans include an academic appointment at the University of Washington, which will allow her to continue focusing on teaching and research, while practicing general internal medicine at the Boise VA Medical Center.

Special education teacher Linda Webb models what she tells her students. "You can learn something. You've just got to believe," she says. "All my life, when I was in that factory and I was working … . It was a job. But it wasn't really what I wanted to do … . I wanted to go back to school. I wanted to prove to myself that I could get that diploma that I didn't get way back then. That was my first goal—to prove to myself that I could do it." Webb's return to school took courage and a lot of hard work, but it opened up an entirely new career. She enjoys the meaningful work of special education that is making a difference in the lives of teenagers. "With God's help there are only abilities, not disabilities," she says. The school where she works is near the school where she completed her GED. "I've made a complete circle," she says.

Webb's academic achievements have influenced her children and grandchildren; she happily ticks off the list of family members who are currently enrolled or have graduated from college since she finished her degrees. "I tell my kids. Learning—that's something that can't be taken away from you."

As for what's next for Webb, "I would love to have my master's degree, but . . . I'm 67," she says, adding her concern about the cost and the fact that her granddaughter is still an undergrad. "But yes," she says softly, "I would like to have my masters. I like learning." She says a diploma for a master's degree would look good hanging on the wall of her office next to the other two diplomas. "You're never too old. It's never too late to be what you might have been."

Through her work with Community Connections, Karen Love improved the lives of many of the over-50 community in Midtown Detroit. "I can look back over my life and see how the hand of God has directed me to where I am now," says Love. "I believe that at this time I am fulfilling the purpose for which I was created."

Not long ago, she helped to launch a new initiative. She is working with the LGBT community and Service and Advocacy for Gay Elders (SAGE) to create a program to promote cultural competency. Social isolation among the LGBT older adult population is significant, says Love. She is collaborating with a SAGE facilitator who will help train the program trainers to implement the initiative throughout the Presbyterian Villages of Michigan. The program will be broadly applicable in reference to diversity and inclusion and will be reproducible through a toolkit. Love hopes the kit will go national. Cultural competency extends beyond the LGBT community, says Love. Some people get uptight if they see someone who is overweight, fixes her hair into an Afro, or wears a veil. Love wants to help people become more accepting of others. "It kind of takes me back to the hippie days where everybody was accepted. They didn't care how you came. They just wanted you to come. I think we've moved away from that freedom of expression of self and loving people."

Although the Community Connections office closed late last summer, Love's efforts to improve the lives of seniors have continued. She currently supervises a project called Senior Reach, part of a national program that supports the wellbeing, independence, and dignity of older adults through community education, mental health services, and connection to community resources. She also leads "Triumph Senior Connection Ministry," an outreach effort based in her church that operates in eight locations throughout Wayne County & Flint. She also continues to work on a small scale at her business, KarYzma Media Consulting. At some point, Love plans to write a book, or two. She is particularly interested in writing about repurposing your life before retiring, a subject she knows on a deeply personal level. For now, Love says she's doing her best to live the most phenomenal "happily ever after" life possible at this stage of her life journey.

"I just want to keep doing what I'm doing," says Cathy. After she graduates, she hopes to expand her home-based career-advising program to help even more young adults. She also plans to continue learning. "I really want to understand adult development more," she says. She finds that parents who bring their children to her for help with career decision-making are often interested in participating in the program too. "They kind of like the idea of having the opportunity to go through this thought process. Also, a lot of people my age are trying to figure out what they want and what they should do next."

Cathy is considering adapting her program for older adults, perhaps developing a three-part workshop, particularly for women, to help them through this process. But the goals will likely be different for this population. They might not be looking for a work option. "A lot of people I know are getting closer to retirement, and they're wondering, 'what am I going to do after retirement? What do I want to spend my time doing? What do I care about?' I really hope I can figure out a program for adults."

Though massage therapy might seem challenging, particularly for someone approaching the age of 70, Stephanie Manriquez claims it is not as physically taxing as it seems if done properly.

"That's the secret. At 50, I came in to massage therapy with two disc repairs and a spinal fusion." She attributes her longevity, 18 years of practice, to using good body mechanics. "I think people our age should not be afraid to do things. Massage helped me discover that." Manriquez cut back gradually on her massage therapy services this past year, maintaining a modest schedule of seven to nine of her regular clients, but she recently announced she's retiring from her home-based business completely.

She also retired from directing the massage therapy program at Central Oregon Community College a couple of years ago but then was invited back to teach courses online part-time. In order to be qualified for online instructing, she had to take a course, one that required a deeper understanding of computers on online processes. "It was not an easy course to take," she says, adding that she completed three rounds of the instruction in order to feel comfortable. She has grown to like the online teaching format. She isn't required to be present in a classroom, but she still feels in touch with students.

With more free time, Manriquez is now enrolled in two classes, one in Spanish and the other in writing, and she is looking at pursuing some long-deferred interests. "I'd like to do watercolor. I'd like to get into better physical shape. I'd like to write. I've always wanted to write a book." She has written several stories based on her family and has an idea for a massage-based work. Her family has grown significantly—by 13 grandchildren. One of her sons expressed concern about his mother cutting back and not having enough to do. Manriquez laughs. "It's been funny."

Manriquez maintains an annual tradition that has become surprisingly predictive of what's to come. Instead of making New Years resolutions, each year at Christmas she writes out a wish list of all she wants in the coming year. Financial, emotional, and physical goals are all fair game. Then she stashes the list away with the Christmas ornaments and forgets about it until the next year. Over the years, this little exercise has surprised her. "When I would open it up and read it, about 75 percent of it had come true." There is something about planting the seed of a wish, she says. She cannot recall exactly what she put on her list this time around, but nearly every year there are wishes related to financial security, good health, and good relations with the family.

Iris Price has put her certifications and degrees to good use. Over the years, she has served as a Feng Shui consultant, designed bookcases and other interior pieces, and applied her understanding of color to enhance living spaces. Price says she has learned a good deal about basic health and the human body. In addition, says Price, "The degree courses taught me how to use these herbs in tinctures, salves, and other ways both topically and internally as medicine, as well as using them in a culinary aspect." Her research skills have served her well in tracking down legitimate information regarding health issues and discerning "quack from fact." Building her knowledge of nutrition, herbs, and essential oils, and gaining understanding of how food affects health and specific disorders has been beneficial to her own health. It also has helped her to become a savvy consumer and a more active participant in her own healthcare. She has caught misinformation; consequently, Price collaborates with practitioners in developing her treatment plans.

While none of Price's courses have been specifically aimed at animals, her chickens, dogs, and especially her goats have also benefited from all she has learned. Her research on diatomaceous earth, which contains fossilized remains of diatoms, a form of hard-shelled algae, led her to employ it in various ways, such as ridding the goats of worms and repelling bugs in the garden. Despite health challenges, Price says she still does almost everything she wants, except she no longer runs half marathons because she dehydrates so rapidly. She still walks for about an hour at a time several days a week and does a little running, and she swims in her backyard pool in warmer months. She consid- ers working in the garden and tending to farm animals as part of her exercise now and doesn't mourn what she is no longer able to do. "I'm happy I was able to do all I did in the past, and now it's onward to different things," she says.

Hanging on a wall in her home office are three framed

certificates from two-year programs, two diplomas for college degrees, and one pink sheet of paper with purple letters that spell out, "Iris P., soon to be, PhD." It's a placeholder for her next diploma. She is looking forward to being called Doctor Iris. "It's never too late," says Price. As for her post-doc plans, she intends to resume writing a health column for the local newspaper, enroll in a free online refresher course in Latin, resume practicing piano and recorder, and re-establish her Renaissance-Baroque music group. And then, who knows? There will always be more to learn.

Completing my MFA was satisfying on a personal level, but once the awareness sunk in that there were no more aca- demic assignments, forms, and deadlines, I felt restless and had an almost overwhelming urge to take on a massive, new project. That is when the idea for this project presented itself, and I am grateful. My hope has always been for my writing to make a difference to someone, somewhere, but there is no assurance whatsoever that anyone, anywhere will be moved or even read the work for that matter. Writing is a humbling process and the product is an act of faith. My favorite writing assignments have always been to tell the stories of people doing good things in hopes of inspiring others or offering a shard of light in a world that at times feels desperate for brightness. In approaching stories such as these, my goal is to write merely with clarity to give the stories center stage. I have found the stories here to be uplifting and inspiring, and I cannot wait to get started on what I have planned next: returning to my MFA thesis, the temporarily abandoned Young Adult novel set in the early 1960s. My main character has been extraordinarily patient, and she is way past due for some resolution to her situation.

Part II

Extending the Learning Life

Chapter 11
Learning as a Lifestyle

"Learning never exhausts the mind."
 – Leonardo da Vinci

Margery Silver, Ed.D., aged 83, has always loved to learn so living on campus suits her. The village she has called home for the past 14 years is affiliated with Lasell College, and each year, residents are required to complete 450 hours of continuing education. For Silver, the obligation to participate in lectures and other educational events is by no means difficult, and her professional background gives her a special understanding of the benefits of lifelong learning. Prior to her retirement at age 78, she was assistant professor of psychology at Harvard Medical School. She also served as associate director of the New England Centenarian Study, investigating cognitive function in individuals of age 100 and over. Silver co-authored *Living to 100: Lessons in Living to Your Maximum Potential at Any Age,* (Basic Books, 1999). "We got a lot of good publicity," says Silver. "I was on the *Oprah Show* and the *Today Show*. It was an exciting new experience."

Silver was drawn to all that Lasell Village had to offer. "As a neuropsychologist I knew scientifically how the brain worked," she says, explaining that challenging the brain builds new pathways to carry information, and many studies show that symptoms of Alzheimer's disease can be delayed even when pathological changes associated with the disease appear in the brain. In the course of her research, fourteen of the centenarians donated their brains to the study, enabling postmortem neuropathological studies to compare with test performance and other evaluations of brain function prior to death. Silver and her colleagues found that even though some of the brains showed pathological signs of Alzheimer's disease, the individuals had been functioning perfectly well in everyday life. "That's because those individuals were lifelong learners in one way or another," says Silver, adding that continued learning enabled them to build critical new pathways so that information could still get through even if a few neurons were damaged.

Since retiring, Silver has settled into a lifestyle centered on learning. "I've always loved going to school," she says. After her freshman year at Barnard, she married a new graduate from Columbia, who was headed for Navy flight training. Three days after the wedding, she started classes at William and Mary and picked up credits at three other colleges as they moved around the country. After six years as a Navy pilot, her husband decided to apply to law school. He was accepted at Harvard, and the couple settled in Boston. Silver finished her undergraduate degree at Simmons College and went to work as an editor for *The Atlantic Monthly*. When her two daughters were young, she free-lanced at home for several publishing houses in Boston. That's when her life took an interesting turn. "I had been editing a lot of textbooks on psychology for Houghton Mifflin," says Silver. "I got much more interested in what I was reading than in the process of editing." When her daughters were in junior high, she decided to go back to school for graduate work in Counseling and Consulting Psychology at Harvard. "I finished my dissertation about two weeks before my fiftieth birthday," says Silver.

For the next ten years, she put her new degree to work as a nursing home consultant. Then along came an opportunity to pursue a post-doctoral fellowship in neuropsychology. After she completed the program, one of her colleagues suggested she talk to Dr. Tom Perls of the New England Centenarian Study at Harvard Medical School and Beth Israel Deaconess Medical Center. Silver joined the study and entered a whole new era of her illustrious career as a researcher in the cognitive functioning of centenarians and a clinician performing neuropsychological evaluations of adults with a specialty in geriatric neuropsychology.

In her late 60s, while Silver was still working full time, she began looking at alternative living situations that offered greater support for her husband who was suffering from Parkinson's Disease. In 2001, the couple moved into Lasell Village, less than a year after the facility opened.

Now that Silver has retired and has more time, she has returned to her literary interests. "I've taken a lot of literature courses. I've taken art, music, film and creative nonfiction," she says. After completing a recent course with an established poet who teaches at the village, her interest in poetry writing has soared. "I just fell in love with it. So that's where my time is going now—to writing poetry." She is taking a poetry workshop off campus and recently had a poem accepted for publication by *Paper Nautilus.*

Silver still has ample opportunity to put her expertise on aging to good use. She's on the Board of Trustees of Lasell Village and on the Medical Advisory Committee. She participates in multigenerational classes and in research at the Fuss Center for Aging and Intergenerational Studies on the Village campus, but her involvement these days is as a subject rather than an investigator.

The learning requirements and its physical location on the college campus distinguish Lasell Village from other university-affiliated retirement communities, says Joann Montepare, Ph.D., Director of Lasell's RoseMary B. Fuss Center for Research on Aging and Intergenerational Studies and Professor of Psychology. "How things are physically set up makes a big difference I think," she says. The 450-hour educational requirement might sound extreme, but the credits refer to the hours spent taking a course, attending a lecture, or participating in a physical activity such as a dance or yoga class, rather than traditional academic credit hours. Those who are still working receive partial credit toward the annual total as well. Residents have the option of enrolling in courses at the college in addition to classes offered at the Village. Residents who have enjoyed successful careers as teachers and professors or have special expertise may also create and teach courses at the Village. In addition, cultural events, concerts, and lectures within the broader community also count toward the requirement. Part of the motivation to live in the Village, says Montepare, is to engage in learning within a college environment simply for the love of it.

The unique relationship between the Village and the college also makes Lasell a natural laboratory to better understand intergenerational interactions and their impact on learning, which is one of the center's research interests. It's more than bringing older residents together with younger residents, says Montepare. She seeks answers to some key intergenerational learning questions: "What's the pedagogical model and how does it work? Are we playing off experience? Are we playing off a group of students who are more diverse?"

Previous research on intergenerational interaction has focused most often on older adults and younger children, and the work in college classrooms has typically centered on students providing services to the older adults in the community in conjunction with courses focused on aging, says Montepare. What we have been interested in is how interactions between individuals of varying ages in the classroom can benefit learning. For instance, in a class on family diversity, what happens if older individuals with broader experience in families participate? Montepare and her colleagues are taking a more systematic look at the kinds of courses that work best to bring different age groups together to determine the extent to which this intergenerational interaction in the classroom actually enhances learning. Calling attention to age can make people self-conscious and provoke thoughts of age stereotypes, which could have a negative effect. Though intergenerational exchanges in academia can often take the form of older adults serving as informants of days past, such as what life was like before computers, Montepare is trying to move away from that model. Instead, she is trying to take age off the table by bringing people together around issues of common interest. By creating learning modules with a specific theme, students of different ages can come together and participate in lectures and discussions, such as a recent forum on transgender identity. Although it's natural for age-related comments to become part of such conversations, when brought into an academic discussion, people tend to see each other as individuals rather than members of specific age groups, says Montepare.

In November 2015, Montepare attended the inaugural Age-Friendly Universities Conference at Dublin City University (DCU) that brought together a group of like-minded professionals from various international institutions of higher education. DCU has taken a lead, laying out age-friendly principles (https://www.dcu.ie/agefriendly/principles.shtml), which Montepare calls "brilliant and perfect." They provide rich guidelines for building a program. We are amid an unprecedentedly massive demographic shift that colleges and universities are not paying a lot of attention to, says Montepare. "Colleges need to provide those older learners with opportunities."

Living on or near campus, like a college student, makes it easy to attend classes. While Lasell's relationship with the Village enjoys the benefits of close physical proximity, other collaborative retirement/education programs exist in various locations throughout the country. The Public Broadcasting System Newshour offers a list of other centers closely affiliated with universities in order to promote lifelong learning: (http://www.pbs.org/newshour/updates/why-boomers-are-retiring-to-college/).

Chapter 12

Teaching and Learning

"To teach is to learn twice."
　　　　　　　　　　– Joseph Joubert

Sharing your knowledge of a subject with others through teaching is a great way to challenge and deepen your own understanding as these next two stories illustrate.

George Pangburn, (MA, Kansas, Geography; MS, Pittsburgh, Energy Resources), aged 66, is passionate about learning and teaching. After retiring about six years ago, he and his wife relocated near Richmond, Virginia. In addition to being near family, the move put them within reach of the Osher Lifelong Learning Institute (OLLI) at the University of Richmond (http://spcs.richmond.edu/osher/). Pangburn was familiar with learning programs that took place in community centers and churches, but he liked the idea of studying with professors affiliated with academic departments. "I knew I wanted to do lifelong learning in an academic setting," says Pangburn.

Launched in 2004, the University of Richmond program has grown to nearly 700 members. Richmond's OLLI is one of 119 Osher Institutes scattered about the country that are affiliated with colleges and universities. Back in 2000, the Bernard Osher Foundation (http://www.osherfoundation.org/index.php?index), pledged its support to develop a national network of programs to promote continued learning after age 50. Classes offered at individual institutes vary. Clicking open the University of Richmond's spring 2016 catalogue revealed an appealing variety of offerings. Among them: *American Crises: Causes, Responses, and Politics; Exploring China from Head to Toe,* and *Bald Eagles of the James River.* Richmond's OLLI students also are able to enroll at a discounted rate in classes at the Center for Culinary Arts.

Prior to retiring, Pangburn served as a senior executive in the U.S. Nuclear Regulatory Commission, managing nuclear safety programs in Rockville, MD, and King of Prussia, PA. He says his former employer "was very big on education and training, particularly for senior executives," which gave him opportunities to attend programs at Harvard, Princeton, and other top-tier universities. He also is a member of the advisory board of the geography department at his alma mater—the University of Kansas. Those academic endeavors only reinforced his commitment to education and provided a foundation for teaching and leading. He now serves as chair of OLLI's Leadership Council, and he was co-chair in developing the program's strategic plan.

Pangburn's academic background is in political geography and nuclear science, but he has taught classes on the Great Plains as well as American foreign policy. He is quick to admit he is not an academic professor, and he feels more like a leader of the class rather than a teacher. Osher members often serve as teachers but the program also brings in current and retired university professors and speakers from the broader community. While most of Richmond's OLLI members enroll in classes specific to the program, they also have the opportunity to audit university courses for a small fee. Members also enjoy some nice perks: access to the university library system, discounts at the campus bookstore, and student dining and theater privileges.

The OLLI classes differ from university classes in that they typically do not require textbooks, individual reading, or advance prep work. Participants show up, listen, take notes, and take part in discussions. "The other thing," says Pangburn, "there are no tests, which is a winning point for many of us." Sometimes, an expert will simply plan a lecture or presentation on a special topic. Not long ago, a reporter and a photographer from the *Richmond Times-Dispatch* presented their experiences in writing and illustrating a book on the back roads of Virginia.

As for Pangburn, the learner, he signs up for 8 to 10 classes per semester. His wife takes courses as well, though they don't always choose the same ones. He often pursues classes in his areas of strong interest, such as history and political science, but he also challenges himself. Each semester, he signs up for at least one "stretch class" focused on a subject he knows little about or has never taken time to explore. A good example is the course he took on the history of music that ran for three semesters, covering everything from caveman melodies to rap and rock and roll. "I love music, but I knew relatively nothing about the history of music…. This was an eye-opener for me; this was a stretch class!"

Beyond his involvement with OLLI, Pangburn has been volunteering within the county government, which has proven to be an additional learning adventure. He joined Senior Ambassadors, a program that teaches individuals age 55 and over about local resources and services in hopes of engaging them in community service. After completing the training, Pangburn became a volunteer on the jury commission that helps select potential jurors for trials in the county.

I must admit, I felt a twinge of envy of those who have access to OLLI programs in their own towns. What an affordable way to continue attending a wide variety of classes. A couple of months after I spoke to George, I discovered through an article in the local newspaper that my very own town in Central Oregon actually hosts an OLLI program offered through the University of Oregon! I was thrilled to discover that classes take place in a facility I had driven past dozens of times. The structure appeared to be only a Duck store that sold products mostly emblazoned with University of Oregon's beloved mascot, but it was also a classroom. I will be enrolling in the program later this year.

Some disciplines, particularly the arts, organically lend themselves to a lifetime of study and effort to achieve mastery. Yet there is still more to know.

Seattle cellist Louie Richmond, MM, aged 73, began playing music at the age of six. He studied cello in college and obtained a master's in music from Temple University. He has an extensive performance background and taught at the college level for five years and offered private lessons for many more. Yet Richmond admits, he is still learning. Among his repertoire are four of Bach's six cello suites; his goal for the coming year is to learn and perform the fifth. Richmond practices with a balance of knowledge and humility: he will never know it all. "You never learn Bach," he says. "You always explore it. You always play it. You always perform it, but you never perfect it."

For Richmond, that's part of what makes music so fascinating. "You never reach perfection. You're always striving for it." But, he adds, "You never get there. That's why music is so great. It's always the process of the journey." The way a piece is played reflects the individual musician's interpretation of the music, which can vary from day to day. "My job is to really find what Bach wanted to say and interpret it in such a way that it's always new and it's always vital and it's never stale," says Richmond. "That's what makes you also want to practice every day because you find new things in something you've played for many years." Because of the complexity of Bach's work, Richmond continues to make new discoveries, particularly in his solo performances. "It's just you and your instrument and no one else, no intermediary," he says. "And that gives you the opportunity to really delve into it and find the secret and how to share that secret with people."

Sharing and teaching music are naturally linked to the learning process, says Richmond. "This is a strange way to look at it but you have 'x' amount of years left, and there's an enormous amount of music that I haven't played or haven't gotten close to playing the way I want it to. I need to spend as much time as possible to learn this music and not only to learn it but to share it with other people."

For the past several years, Richmond has been sharing his music with residents of senior living centers, even playing at the bedside of those too ill to attend performances for larger audiences. He now serves as the volunteer music director for Village Concepts University, a new program within a network of assisted living facilities that allows residents to take credit courses on site. Richmond's concerts are nourishing for both the mind and the spirit, and his approach to teaching classical music is refreshing. "I make it very informal," he says. "One of the major problems with classical music: it's so stuffy… It doesn't need to be formal." He invites the audience to ask questions and tries to keep the atmosphere relaxed so attendees do not feel intimidated. And above all, says Richmond, "[I] never play down to people." He plays music that he would perform on any stage in the world. "I treat them with the respect of any audience because they're giving up to me what is the most valuable thing in the world—their time. By them giving me an hour of their time, I have to make it valuable for them or they're not coming back," says Richmond.

It's the same approach he took in teaching college. Richmond taught electives, which meant, "If I didn't teach well, the students didn't sign up for the classes." The process of teaching deepened his understanding of music as well. "It's a dual learning experience." He feels strongly about teachers and students learning simultaneously, contending, "If they're not learning, they shouldn't be teaching."

Richmond is always interested in finding better ways to share music with people. Given his extensive performance experience, which includes playing with the National Symphony Orchestra, sharing music is second nature. He started the Northwest Chamber Orchestra, an organization that lasted many years. These days, he can easily hold four concerts in a week, which means he is continuously practicing, always preparing for the next performance. He often performs with a pianist, a retired physician who shares Richmond's love of playing music, and he plays with some chamber music groups.

"I think there's a lot of people my age who feel we're not here just to watch TV or reminisce about careers…we want to do something for ourselves," says Richmond. There is something about playing music that transcends age, he says. "You just try to do it as best as possible. You're ageless. I don't want people to see me as a 73-year old cellist…. I want them to see me as a cellist. That's all. And that's the great thing about music and the great thing about learning. It really levels the playing field. It doesn't matter how old you are. You just want to learn."

In his current role working with seniors, age gives him an

advantage. He can better relate to those he teaches. "We have some shared experiences," he says. There is also a great appreciation for his work. Sometimes seven or eight people will be gathered early, waiting for Richmond to arrive. "It's very good for your ego," he says. "People rely on you and that's exciting. You feel needed and it's very good to feel needed. No matter how old you are; no matter what competency level you are at. It's a good feeling."

Richmond recently retired from his own public relations firm, giving him more time to focus on music. He launched Richmond Public Relations (http://richmondpublicrelations.com/) 23 and a half years ago, a firm now run by his son. At the time, he was a fairly well known musician and college teacher, but he says, "I just wasn't making a lot of money." As Richmond considered options, he realized that all his travels as a musician had given him a solid understanding of the hotel industry. "I thought if I could start an orchestra, if I could teach electives, maybe I could do public relations for hotels." Richmond admits he was lucky in getting his foot in the door. The woman in charge of hiring the public relations director prior to the opening of the Alexis Hotel just happened to be a classical music aficionado. She hired Richmond. "There I was in a new world of public relations and honestly not knowing what to do," he recalls. It was the early '80s, before desktop computers, and Richmond arrived for work to find beautiful offices, a staff of secretaries, and his first task—to write the marketing plan. "I didn't know what to do." At first, he says, "I just panicked." But then he considered the skills he had used to launch an entire orchestra—skills and experience that were applicable to the new position. He spent two years at the Alexis then served as the director of public relations for the Sheraton for eight more. When he turned 50, he decided to break away and launch his own firm. "It just seemed like the right thing to do," he says. The Sheraton joined him and remains a client to this day.

Richmond doesn't think of himself as retired. "Retired is a weird word," he says. "I see myself as a career-changer. I'm really busy now. I'm really working hard. I'm not working hard at public relations; I'm just doing something different." Richmond says retirement often has a negative connotation. "I have some friends who still work because they're scared of quitting, because they have absolutely nothing to do," he says. He feels it's important to cultivate interests earlier in life rather than wait until the sixth or seventh decade. "You can't wait until you retire to find an interest. It's too late, and it could be that you don't do it that well, and it's really frustrating because you know how it should be," says Richmond.

When he's not practicing or performing, Richmond is likely to be running. He runs 40 to 50 miles a week and has completed 50 marathons, running his first at age 40. He plans to do the next one after turning 75, which will put him into a new age bracket for competing. As for his secret to logging so many miles without injury: "I'm slow," he says. "Running is very important to me, it's a very important part of my life. It really helps clear my head." But Richmond also admits he runs simply to enjoy himself.

It's a sentiment that echoes the motivation behind his music. He says, "I do it for the joy."

Chapter 13
Fulfilling a Dream

"Every great dream begins with a dreamer."
– Harriet Tubman

"If anyone told me I'd still be writing at this age I would have said you've got to be kidding." Back in her earlier years, Sylvia Lieberman, aged 98, had a dream of one day seeing a piece of her own writing appear on a shelf in Barnes and Noble. Throughout much of her life, the native New Yorker has taken writing-related classes at various colleges, including New York University and The New School. Over the years, she has studied journalism, advertising, publicity, radio and television, script writing and fashion writing. While taking a course called "Writing for the Juvenile Reader," Lieberman's work got noticed. The instructor directed the class to write a story about the adventures of a small animal. Instead of writing about cuddly puppies, kittens, or bunnies, Lieberman decided to write a story about a mouse named Archibald. When the professor returned her manuscript, Lieberman looked for the critiques and comments that typically appeared in the margins. Instead, a little note appeared at the top of the first page: "This material is publishable. See me after class." The professor handed her a list of children's book publishers. Lieberman was thrilled. Two days later her excitement came to an abrupt halt. Her father died unexpectedly. She filed away her manuscript and forgot about it.

Several years later, Lieberman suffered another devastating loss. Her husband passed away unexpectedly at the age of 55. Then 50, Lieberman was in shock for a long time. Somehow two whole years slipped by. Meanwhile, her daughter had dream taking shape as well—to become a physician. "I hadn't worked for 25 years," Lieberman recalls. "I just had to do something …

not just sit home and cry." She pulled herself together, got a job managing a doctor's office, and enrolled in night classes. She wasn't interested in going to school for a degree. "As long as I was learning, as long as I was progressing in my writing, that made me happy," she says.

Lieberman's daughter became a physician, began practicing in Beverly Hills, and had a daughter of her own. She also found a special way to thank her mom for supporting her dream—by finding a publisher for *Archibald's Swiss Cheese Mountain*, (Seven Locks Press, 2007). When the book was in print, the publisher arranged for an initial book signing. It took place at Barnes and Noble. As Lieberman approached the store, she saw a sign out front that read: *Book Signing and Reading—1 p.m. by author Sylvia Lieberman, public invited.* Lieberman recalls the smile that spread across her face as she entered the store. Her dream had come true.

For the next three and a half years, Lieberman, in the company of her beloved Archibald, enjoyed additional signings and readings. She gave interviews for articles, radio programs, and television. She participated in book festivals and even rode a float in the Hollywood Christmas parade. The book received a number of awards, including Best Children's Book Award (2008) at both the Hollywood Book Festival and the London Book Festival.

Six years ago, Lieberman relocated to California and was delighted to discover a new avenue for continuing her studies and growing as a writer: College Emeritus, a program of Santa Monica College geared to mature students. (http://www.smc. edu/academicaffairs/emeritus/Pages/default.aspx). The program launched in 1975, and offers about 120 free classes for more than 3,000 students annually.

Lieberman has taken various classes over the past four years and frequently attends special lectures put on by professors and instructors affiliated with nearby UCLA. At Emeritus, Lieberman has concentrated her studies on writing autobiography. The coursework naturally extends beyond the classroom in the form of homework, but she doesn't mind. She is in the process of writing her life story. Each year, some of the student work is selected for inclusion in an annual publication that serves as a fundraiser for the program. Lieberman is pleased that her written work has been selected for the past four issues.

She admits the technology aspect of writing, typing on a keyboard and viewing her words on a computer screen, is a problem due to macular degeneration. But she works around it. She writes her stories by hand then turns them over to her daughter or her granddaughter for word processing.

Lieberman completed two more Archibald stories at her publisher's request, but the company went out of business before the works went to press. She's concerned about the changes in the book industry and the subsequent closure of so many bookstores. Back when she was signing copies of *Archibald*, she remembers the aisles of the stores being filled with shoppers. Now, she says, they can stay home, push a button, and get a book, and a lot of people are self-publishing.

For now, Lieberman continues to write and indulge her love of learning. She can't see any other kind of life. "It's just enjoyable."

It seems to me Sylvia Lieberman is an inspiration for writers of any age and a model of persistence, a critical component in the writing business. I understand on a personal level the desire to write our life stories, and I wonder if that urge in some of us might grow stronger, more urgent, with age. Over the past few decades, I have found numerous ways of learning more about the art, the craft, and the business of writing and ways to live the writing life. Fortunately, being older and having an abundance of life experience is an invaluable resource for a writer. Bizarre backgrounds, unexpected events, odd perspectives, and failure at just about anything make for good raw material; it's what an individual writer makes of such stuff that ultimately matters. Failed attempts at anything in life often make more interesting stories than perfect outcomes. For instance, rather than read about a perfect holiday on a sun-soaked beach, I much prefer to delve into a travel story about a family that ends up camping in the woods beneath a t-shirt tent, dining on potato-chip soup, and telling stories all night because Dad preferred to wing it instead of using a map or a GPS or stopping to ask for directions.

Writing is always on my list of subjects to continue studying, and I feel certain I would benefit from pretty much any kind of educational venture that prompts a deeper, broader look at the world. But I have also found writing-focused courses and workshops to be invaluable, even if purely for the chance to receive feedback on work and to interact with a community of like-minded people. While colleges and universities typically provide a broader range of options for writing in specific genres, such as poetry, fiction, and creative nonfiction, writing workshops and author lectures can be found within local libraries, senior centers, and other organizations.

Larger cities boast festivals, like Chicago with its annual Printer's Row Lit Festival, and New Orleans, which offers both the Tennessee Williams/New Orleans Literary Festival and the Words and Music Literary Festival each year. These are great opportunities to listen to panels of authors talk about writing and their work.

A couple of years ago, I joined a very active writing community called the Central Oregon Writer's Guild, (http://www. centraloregonwritersguild.com). This group supports writers in a variety of ways, including coordinating genre-specific critique groups, disseminating information and opportunities of interest to writers, challenging writers to produce new work to submit to an annual writing contest, and hosting seminars on such topics as self-publishing. I've also found an abundance of online resources for writers who want to learn more about anything and everything related to writing or who just want the companionship of an online community of writers. In fact, there are so many out there, writers are wise to be selective in choosing only the forums that serve their needs. Otherwise, there is a very real risk of having no time left to write! Annually, I scope out *Writer's Digest* with its an annual list of "101 Best Websites for Writers" to see if anything new appeals to me. The list includes sites to nurture creativity, learn how to approach publishers and agents, avoid scams, and find genre-specific discussion groups.

More informally, in my endless quest to continue learning to improve my work, I have assembled an embarrassingly large collection of books on all things related to writing. I also keep a file of articles clipped from decades-old issues of writing periodicals. Which leads to another important learning strategy—reading. 'Good writers are usually good readers' is an often-repeated theme among writers.

I also believe in the good old-fashioned "writer's group" to push productivity—as long as the members are kind, supportive, and congenial. The first writing group I joined many years ago, never really got off the ground in terms of peer review. Years later, I became part of another group of about six writers in New Orleans who were serious about producing new material, providing thoughtful but kind critiques, and submitting work for publication. Collectively, we successfully published essays, short stories, poems, and even a novel. Unfortunately, Hurricane Katrina came along and some of us relocated. How I miss that writing group!

The other aspect of writing that I think deserves mentioning, especially given the specific focus of this collection. I believe writing is also a way of learning. After I have written on a subject, I feel as if I have gained a deeper understanding. I knew something about subjects like bullying, mosquito-borne diseases, art as a form of therapy, and fundraising, but then I wrote about them, which took me on a deeper journey of discovery. The same is true for seemingly ordinary day-to-day experiences like pulling weeds, making a school lunch, thinking of a pair of 30-year-old figure skates as "new." Writing on these topics gave me the opportunity to look at them differently and far more intensely, to make connections, and to remember and discover aspects of life I hadn't noticed before or thought I had forgotten. This strikes me as a way of using the mind and the imagination to learn something new—and it requires no classes, money, or Internet connection. It's self-directed, which makes for a good transition to the next chapter and reflects the possibilities for carving your own path of learning discovery.

Chapter 14

Creating Your Own Course of Study

"O for a Muse of fire, that would ascend the brightest heaven of invention."
— William Shakespeare
(*Henry V*, Act I, Chorus)

Education can evolve a passion into an area of expertise, sometimes with a minimum of effort. However, when the subject of study depends on the senses for full comprehension, it presents an interesting challenge that relies on individual sensitivity and perception to deliver a portion of the learning material.

Mark Lindner, MLS, aged 57, has achieved proficiency in two distinctly different fields: library science and beer. Occasionally, the two overlap. Lindner's understanding of library resources and research strategies serves him well, particularly as he continues to delve more deeply into the scientific and anthropological aspects of a brew that is downright beloved in his hometown of Bend, Oregon.

Lindner obtained his Masters in Library Science from the University of Illinois at Urbana-Champaign in his late 40s, after retiring from a twenty-year career in the U.S. Army. Since turning 50, Lindner has continued learning by taking a variety of college courses and community education classes, pursuing online certifications, and doing lots of reading. He works part-time as a librarian at Central Oregon Community College (COCC). Since he and his wife, also a librarian, moved here in 2012, Lindner has taken advantage of the college's wealth of community learning courses, particularly those offered through the school's Culinary Institute. In addition to cooking classes, he completed a sensory analysis class in how to taste beer as well as introductory courses in all-grain brewing. "I've also been working on some various certifications," says Lindner. Through online work and self-study, he obtained certification as a Cicerone Certified Beer Server; he also holds a Beer Steward certificate from the Master Brewer's Association of the Americas. Lindner is currently set to begin a serious course of study to become certified as a beer judge. The examination process is a tier system, requiring him to pass an online test of 200 questions in sixty minutes in order to qualify for the next level of evaluation.

Lindner also writes about beer on his blog, the Bend Beer Librarian (http://marklindner.info/bbl/) and in other venues, and he is a member of the North American Guild of Beer Writers. Prior to relocating to Oregon, much of his post-50 learning focused on writing and poetry. His wife served as a librarian at Briar Cliff University, which came with tuition benefits for spouses. Lindner says, "It was interesting because there were all these classes I had avoided for 50 years." He seized the opportunity to make up for lost time. He took about a dozen classes over a two-year period that included courses in Victorian Literature, British Literature, fairy tales, mad women poets, grammar, and writing. He started writing poetry and took a class in digital photography, often pairing photos with his written work.

Lindner has made wise use of tuition benefits throughout his adult life. While in the Army, he completed an Associate of Arts degree along with additional courses for credit. As long as he passed the course, the Army covered much of the tuition. Though he attended various schools as he moved about, the institutions were all part of a network of colleges and universities that agree to accept credits from other members as service to the military population. "That was nice," says Lindner. "It protected you in that way."

After retiring from the army in 1998, he took a staff position in a library and attended Illinois State University to complete his Bachelor's Degree in Philosophy. Then it was on to graduate school to study library and information science at the University of Illinois at Urbana-Champaign. Though Lindner didn't use federal money to offset costs, he did take advantage of the Illinois Veterans Grant, which provided four years of tuition benefits. After completing his master's degree, Lindner continued to study and, by 2009, had finished coursework for a second degree in library science with a different focus. But non-academic aspects of his life moved to the forefront—he was getting married and preparing to relocate.

In addition to tuition benefits, the military service gave him the opportunity to live in Germany and Belgium—two countries well suited to better understanding beer. Lindner has done a lot of independent reading on the anthropological aspects of beer and the various ways of making it, such as the South American chicha approach of chewing and spitting corn to enable the fermentation process and African chibuku developed from sorghum and maize. One of the ways he builds his knowledge is by paying attention to citations in the literature. He admits to being an inveterate footnote tracker—one text leads to another or sometimes, many others. Lindner says it's a great way to build knowledge in a particular field. His knowledge of library systems is a great help in tracking down obscure sources. "There are a few things I'd like to get my hands on that are only at the Library of Congress and Anheuser-Busch," says Lindner. He hasn't yet used his knowledge to do his own brewing. "I've helped people a few times. I haven't done it myself." For now, he says, "I want to keep learning things. Keep taking classes and studying things on my own."

Art relies heavily on carving your own path, finding your own way. You might learn the fundamentals of drawing and various techniques through coursework, but when it comes to expressing that knowledge in a tangible form, what lives within the mind, heart, and spirit can transform learning into something unique. That internal artistic influence is perhaps a force to be discovered rather than studied. Such discovery might well spark a vision for something new, an art form that has never been done before, which requires the artist to turn to invention and perhaps a bit of trial and error, to learn what works and what doesn't.

Back when Jack Beckstrom, B.A., J.D., LL.M, M.A., aged 83, was six years old, someone snapped a photo of him standing beside the sculptor of Mt. Rushmore who was instructing a team of stonecutters heading up to work on the presidents' faces. The image was a foreshadowing of Beckstrom's life after 50.

In middle school, tests placed Beckstrom in the top one percent of the population for eye/hand coordination, which suggested he had an aptitude for art. But before Beckstrom reached the fifth decade of life, he had little time for art. His few artistic creations included a handful of drawings, a painting he gave to a landlady, and a statue of an oversized, metal Santa riding a giant drone bee placed at the entrance of an Air Force base in Florida during a holiday season.

Today, Beckstrom's sculptures fill a gallery in downtown Chicago (http://www.beckstromgallery.com/). But these are not ordinary sculptures or pieces that can be fully appreciated within the typical token gallery pause, which Beckstrom says, is an average of four seconds. The works are, without exception, complex. Months after seeing the collection, the pieces are still on my mind, particularly, the nude couple sitting in a garden, smoking and snacking with their imperfect bodies perfectly rendered, and the six dynamic figures in "Fainting at the Costume Ball" whose costumes are as mesmerizing as the characters' dramatic facial expressions.

"I'm a storytelling sculptor," says Beckstrom, surrounded by 23 years of his work. "It's a career here . . . I made a niche for myself of this storytelling and I filled up the niche." Literary works such as *A Midsummer Night's Dream* and *Cyrano de Bergerac* inspire some of the compositions while life's beautiful and tragic moments are reflected in others. "This is what I was born to do," says Beckstrom. "I didn't fully realize it until I started to do it." But Beckstrom got a late start. "I was side-tracked," he says. "I lost my way."

Beckstrom started out as an art major at Lawrence College, now Lawrence University. But his freshman year was loaded with core requirements, allowing him to take only one drawing class.

After the first year, the University of Iowa lured him away with the offer of a partial scholarship to play tennis, and Beckstrom ended up majoring in political science and minoring in English. It was the time of the Korean War, and Beckstrom was enrolled in the Reserve Officers' Training Corps (ROTC), which allowed him to finish college without being drafted. After graduating, he was commissioned into the Air Force for two years of active duty. In those days, the AF-ROTC program allowed a choice between either training to become a pilot, which came with a four-year service obligation, or serving as a ground officer, which reduced the commitment to two years. Beckstrom planned to attend law school after active duty, so he opted for the latter. Two of his college roommates, however, chose to become pilots. Both died in non-combat plane crashes before the age of 30.

After active duty, Beckstrom remained in the reserves for six years and attended the University of Iowa School of Law. He had originally planned to stay in Iowa and join his wife's family friend in practice, but graduating at the top of his class gave him more opportunities. He interviewed with a few top firms and accepted an offer from former New York governor Thomas Dewey, a named partner of a large Wall Street law firm. Dewey had been the republican candidate for president on two runs, losing in 1944 to Franklin D. Roosevelt and in 1948 to Harry S. Truman. Beckstrom worked at the firm for five years and discovered he didn't particularly like corporate law. "I liked what I like to call people law, mom and pop law, estates and trusts, family law, and so forth," says Beckstrom.

So he moved the family to Rockford, Illinois, and settled into a nice little law firm where a former tennis mentor of his worked. That lasted seven months. "I'd gotten bitten by the big city bug," says Beckstrom. "I realized I couldn't live in a city that small for the rest of my life." His New York law firmed welcomed him back. After a couple of years, he decided that maybe his future was in academia. He entered a teaching fellowship program at Harvard Law School that allowed him to study, to teach first-year law students part-time, and to earn a Masters Degree in Law

(LL.M). When the deans of various law schools came recruiting, Beckstrom received a couple of invitations to interview. He accepted a teaching position at Northwestern University School of Law, located in downtown Chicago where he could continue to enjoy the perks of a large city.

The academic environment presented new opportunities. In the late 1960s, Beckstrom was into his second year at Northwestern, when a member of the sociology department invited him to collaborate on a grant project that focused on fostering communication between diverse societies. Beckstrom developed an African-based project that stretched over a two-year period and involved American law students doing field work with Ethiopian law students to study the legal system in Ethiopia. The project resulted in numerous collaborative journal articles. Beckstrom continued to focus on this work as a visiting scholar at the University of London on a post-graduate Fulbright scholarship. His wife and two children accompanied him, and by the end of the year, he had earned another master's degree.

Life remained busy for the tenured law professor, but as he reached his fifties, shortly after his marriage ended, Beckstrom's desire to develop his artistic side grew more urgent. "I realized if I was going to do anything with art, I had better get with it," he says. He joined the Palette and Chisel, an organization in downtown Chicago that has been supporting the development of artists since 1895 (http://www.paletteandchisel.org/). "The first year I just drew," Beckstrom recalls. He spent most nights and one day on the weekends sketching models during open studio sessions. "I got my fill of drawing," he says. "The next year, I painted." Though today, numerous artists teach a wide-range of courses at the organization, including sculpting, when Beckstrom joined, there was only one instructor who taught painting. There was no sculpting instruction. "I took the painting course and just had ten sessions, one a week for ten weeks," he says. But one day, Beckstrom happened to be at the facility and saw someone sculpting during an open studio when everyone else was either drawing or painting. "I said to myself, 'I can do that too.'"

The following week, he tracked down a life-sized, human écorché (skinless statue) and brought it into the studio space he rented from the Palette and Chisel and went to work sculpting a version that was one-third of the life-size statue. "That's the first thing I ever did," says Beckstrom, and what he learned from creating that first sculpture was the kind of profound self-discovery that is life-changing. His critical eye told him the piece was as good as the work of established artists he'd seen and appreciated. Beckstrom recalls, "I said if I can do that I can do anything."

He admits his story is a little different. Beckstrom didn't seem to need formal art instruction. "I had it in my system already," he says. "I was born with it. I have a lot of patience. It's not really an intelligence. It's something else—determination and patience. This sounds egotistical and maybe improbable, but the first thing I ever did was as good as the last thing I did. The difference was that the original pieces took longer to get right—to finish."

After that first sculpture, he went to the dean of the law school and said, "I need to get out of teaching law." The dean told him it would take a year to find a replacement to which Beckstrom replied, "Let's get the process started." A year later, Beckstrom was sculpting at the Palette and Chisel full time. He worked on busts, including one of the dean of Northwestern Law School. Beckstrom sculpted the piece by referencing a series of photos of his subject taken from various angles.

Though Beckstrom had a minimal amount of formal education in art of any sort, he learned about various sculpting techniques on his own by reading, and he visited most of the major art museums in the Western world. Beckstrom believes you can learn a lot about the mechanics of sculpting by reading books, but he says, "They can't teach you the touch." When it came to actually creating work, his approach was relatively simple: "I didn't stop until it looked exactly, to my mind, like the subject." Says Beckstrom, "I'm not the brightest person around, but I have something that not many people have, which is really intense determination, will power, and high tolerance for pain and discomfort. "It made sense for me just to keep sculpting until I finished the project"

The three-dimensional aspect of the sculpture form is one of the great challenges. "You can't get caught up in one angle," says Beckstrom. "It's a beginner's fault." He often sees students begin sculpting and get all concerned with a single detail, like an eye, and refuse to move until it's perfect. "That's wrong," he says, "You have to go to the next eye and develop it somewhat, then around to the ear for a while, and then the ear on the other side and keep moving around." These days, the Palette and Chisel has open studios with models specifically for sculptors, but that wasn't the case when Beckstrom began sculpting. He often used a series of enlarged photos to work from. Eventually, he developed an approach to turning a series of photos into a video segment to create more life-like references.

"We started very primitively," says Beckstrom. His son Blake, who is a video producer, helped gather the equipment and develop the approach. "It was really complicated stuff," says Beckstrom. He learned by trial and error, working through several stages to perfect a system that enabled him to use a camera connected to a television, take photos of a model from every angle, and broadcast it onto the screen. This allowed Beckstrom to sculpt from the virtual 360-degree views using images of the subject viewed on the television.

The approach became particularly important to his storytelling compositions. "I get a story in mind, and I picture how the actors in the story would be situated—what their pose would be—and then I go and find appropriate models for that and take pictures all around them," says Beckstrom. A few of his models are family members. His son, daughter, and daughter-in-law have all served as models. And Beckstrom has often called on a grandson at different ages. "Every time I needed a kid, I used him because he's cheap," Beckstrom laughs.

For many of his pieces, Beckstrom used terra alba, a natural type of clay that fires to a pure white. Other work has been bronzed, an expensive process that requires the original clay piece to be sacrificed. Though Beckstrom learned on his own about these processes, when it came to trying his hand at sculpting marble, he figured he needed some guidance. He studied with Omri Amrany, a sculptor in Highland Park, IL. Amrany and his wife, Julie Rotblatt-Amrany sculpted a well-known piece called "The Spirit," a larger-than-life size bronze sculpture of Michael Jordan that stands outside the United Center where the Chicago Bulls play. Beckstrom commuted to Highland Park for an entire summer to learn reduction sculpture, which mostly involves using baby jackhammers to whittle away at a chunk of marble. The result of that effort is a stunning bust of Beckstrom's daughter, but he found the process very unforgiving. Remove a little too much marble from one spot and there's no means to correct it. "You've got to go very, very slowly," says Beckstrom, "It's precarious … it's not worth the effort."

Beckstrom returned to his story-telling work that grew increasingly complex. Around the time he turned 80, he had created a body of work that amounted to an entire career. "I really did everything I wanted to do in terms of storytelling, then I thought, what should I do now?" I decided to start a new series—women as wild animals. He sculpted a half-lizard/half-woman piece and a figure that was part jaguar/part woman. But Beckstrom wasn't happy with the pieces. He decided to work on another complex composition of 12 to 14 figures on a raft, based on *The Raft of the Medusa,* a painting by French artist Théodore Géricault that depicts the aftermath of a shipwreck near the African coast. To stage the scene, he set up a collection of movable wooden figures, but before he started sculpting, Beckstrom had second thoughts. "I said 'man this is crazy! You're going to spend a year and a half or two years to sculpt this and if it ever got into a gallery, people would pass it by. It's too complicated. They wouldn't care to give it the time to figure it out." With that awareness and the fact that he had already filled a gallery with work, Beckstrom decided he had done enough sculpting.

He still maintains a studio and serves as vice president of the Palette and Chisel. He wrote a book that reflects what he learned through the years about sculpting: *Making Art by Jack: Jack Beckstrom's No Nonsense Guide and Commentary—Including the*

New Way to Sculpt. This was the fourth book Beckstrom authored. His other three titles are: *Sociobiology and the Law,* (University of Illinois Press, 1985); *Evolutionary Jurisprudence,* (University of Illinois Press, 1989); and *Darwinism Applied: Evolutionary Paths to Social Goals,* (Praeger, 1993).

Last year, Beckstrom challenged himself in an entirely new way. He has no background in music, but he's always wanted to be able to play *Stardust*, a 1927 composition of Hoagy Carmichael. So, he signed up for piano lessons, bought a portable keyboard for practice, and told the instructor of his goal. She started out teaching him the fundamentals and assigning him 30 minutes of practice time every day. Beckstrom kept at it for two months, but then spring came along, bringing with it the biking season. He told the instructor he wasn't signing up for the next session because he was heading back to bicycling. He admits it was a crutch excuse. "The real reason was I didn't want to work that hard anymore, particularly at something that I wasn't intrinsically interested in," he says. "I wasn't ready to be that kind of student anymore."

These days, Beckstrom spends his days working out and staying fit, alternating days of cardio workouts with days of strengthening exercises, and of course, biking when weather permits. "The rest of the time I'm reading novels," he says. During the past three or four years, he has read the novels considered the top 25 of the 21st Century, and he has plans to read his way through other lists of literary works by Pulitzer and Nobel Prize winning authors. "My days are full and I have no desire to do anymore art," says Beckstrom. "I did it."

Even Michelangelo reached an endpoint to his work. Beckstrom describes the "Master's" pieces that were left incomplete. Some people have interpreted the unfinished pieces as Michelangelo's final statement on how to sculpt, but Beckstrom speculates: "He was just tired and gave it up." Despite his late start, Beckstrom says he is lucky he got started when he did—in his 50s. It gave him 23 years to create and to complete the work he set out to do. "It fulfilled me."

Chapter 15
More Options to Explore

"Knowledge the wing wherewith we fly to heaven."

– William Shakespeare
(*Henry VI*, Act IV, Scene 7)

While I suspect few readers will have any trouble coming up with their own list of resources to satisfy their learning needs and plans, I share here a few more ideas that might be interesting to explore. By no means are these offerings intended to be comprehensive and programs specifically described are merely ideas, perhaps suggesting a launching point for a personal search. Online learning alone is vast and ever changing. What was Googleable today might be gone tomorrow. Similarly, educational possibilities that can only be imagined today might become next year's hot new academic program available in App form.

Thanks to the online world, we now have access to a virtual learning candy store. I recently had some fun visiting the online learning site www.udemy.com that claims you can find a course on anything. I decided to test it. I found courses in sewing, dog grooming, and web design. And while there are no classes on corn shucking, there are plenty of offerings to learn about gardening. If you're looking for single classes like these, tracking down just the right one can be great fun. Other programs, however, might demand a bit more research.

Before signing up for an online program, particularly one that leads to a degree, it's wise to undertake a bit of due diligence. Learn about the organization. Is it accredited and if so, by what agency? Is it non-profit or for profit? Devon Haynie's article for the *U.S. News and World Report* offers some guidance for appraising institutions that offer online degree-seeking programs: (https://www.usnews.com/education/online-education/ articles/2015/06/09/7-warning-signs-an-online-degree-is-a-scam).

But that's enough of the scary stuff. This chapter is offered as a bit of brainstorming about possible learning resources not only online, but also within the community. These are but a handful of examples and ideas, with a few personal favorites thrown in. Another learner might develop an entirely different list of resources that bears no resemblance to what I provide here.

Before shifting away from university offerings, it is worth mentioning that many institutions of higher education offer special programs specifically for the broader community that are purely educational and cost little or nothing. Community theater productions, mini-medical schools, and brown bag lunches are just a few of the outreach activities I have encountered (and sometimes planned) during the more than ten years I worked in higher ed. Additionally, numerous college-level courses, both for credit and noncredit, can be found online. One such resource, the Massive Open Online Course (MOOC) site (https://www.mooc-list. com/), makes for fun browsing. It provides open (free) access to courses offered by both universities as well as other providers, usually for no credit, though some do offer certifications. The site is searchable by subject, providing institution, instructor, and language and the offerings vary widely. Other sites worth surfing for free and low-cost courses include: Lynda (http://www.lynda. com/), Udacity (https://www.udacity.com/), edX (https://www. edx.org/), and Khan Academy (https://www.khanacademy.org/). At codeacademy (https://www.codecademy.com/), you can sign up for interactive courses to learn how to write code.

A couple of other websites worth mentioning: Coursera (www.coursera.org/) offers online courses from various universities, including international partners. And Classroom 2.0 Live (http://live.classroom20.com/) provides a learning forum that offers educational opportunities through webinars and real-time participation in presentations and discussions. For anyone who has never tried webinars, the site gives detailed instruction on how to get started using the technology and format.

These days, a number of prestigious institutions are sharing many of their courses, free of charge, with a world of learners. I recently listened to a lecture called "Sensing Place: Photography as Inquiry" offered at MIT (https://ocw.mit.edu/index.htm). Shortly thereafter, I discovered a presentation on "Hemingway, Fitzgerald, Faulkner" provided by Open Yale Courses (http://oyc.yale.edu/). I'm considering participating in a class at Stanford (https://lagunita.stanford.edu/) called "Language, Proof, and Logic" because the course promo featured two instructors who make it clear that this will be a fun forum for learning. Though there is a $55 fee for materials for this specific class, most of the site's offerings are free. Best College Reviews offers a listing and summary of numerous other similar online learning opportunities (http://www.bestcollegereviews.org/).

I recently learned of MasterClass (www.masterclass.com/) that permits studying with the stars. Study acting through an online class with Kevin Spacey or Dustin Hoffman and learn photography from Annie Leibovitz.

Certain subjects are best learned through first-hand experience. The Road Scholar (www.roadscholar.org/) marries education to travel. This non-profit organization offers worldwide programs geared to mature adults and intergenerational learners. The organization, previously called Elderhostel, has been in operation since 1975 and offers more than 5,000 educational tours with destinations, including all 50 states and 150 countries. The educational component of the programs focus on a wide range of subjects, ranging from investigating endangered whooping cranes in Port Aranas, Texas, to rediscovering Shakespeare on a voyage between London and Dublin. Road Scholar engages local educators and experts who know their subjects and the area and culture as well. The organization also offers special intergenerational programs. And it supports more than 400 Lifelong Learning Institutes across the country in providing educational programs in a range of disciplines, including arts, sciences, society, business, and technology.

A few other subjects, such as yoga, art, music, and dance, might be easier to learn by being physically present, face-to-face with the instructor and fellow students, at least initially. Although, if you want to build a base knowledge before showing up to class or if you just like the freedom of attending a session at your convenience, there are plenty of courses available on DVD. I have attended yoga classes on DVD for years.

Joining a class in the arts as an adult beginner can be particularly challenging and even if ultimately it proves to be something you would rather not continue, no learning experience is ever a waste in my opinion. A new educational experience has a way of broadening the world and providing a fresh perspective, which can inform and benefit other aspects of life. As a painter, I had only ever been a dabbler until I had the post- Hurricane Katrina opportunity to study at two small arts organizations—The New Orleans Academy of Fine Art and The Palette and Chisel Academy of Fine Art in Chicago. After completing several courses, not only had I gained a better understanding of the techniques and materials used in drawing, watercolor, and oil painting, I started seeing details about the world that I had not previously noticed. Painting a subject forced me to study it, which had the broader impact of pushing me to open my eyes wider and look longer and harder at everything around me. I now find greater appreciation of the nuances of color. A barn isn't just red anymore--it's cadmium red with a dab of viridian and a smidge of titanium white.

Living in a remote location might make the hunt for such on-site classes more difficult; on the other hand, the perfect class might be right around the corner in a business or studio. I had passed by an interesting old warehouse-style building in Bend, Oregon, a dozen times or so before I finally took the time to stop in and investigate. I was delighted to find a small community of creative and artistic people hard at work in this uniquely transformed space called The Workhouse (http://www.theworkhouse-bend.com/). The artists worked even as shoppers strolled by and interrupted periodically to ask questions. Some of the artists also teach their crafts, allowing members of the community to try something new, like painting with beer and coffee or up cycling a pile of junk into jewelry. Seeing a version of Vermeer's "Girl with a Pearl Earring" rendered with coffee as the main medium serves to expand the possibilities for this common brew.

Similar classes and activities might be found in the YMCA, churches, community or senior centers, possibly at a lower cost. One example of a vibrant organization is The New Orleans Jewish Community Center (www.nojcc.org/), which sits at the heart of Uptown New Orleans. The place is buzzing with activity, including adult classes of all sorts and a lecture series covering diverse topics such as "The Evolution of Women in the Legal Profession" and "Housing Equity." There is even a series of weekly classes called "Mind Matters" that focus on keeping the memory sharp.

Not to be overlooked as a significant community resource for education is the ordinary, but often extraordinary, local library. I admit to getting a bit sentimental over libraries for a couple of reasons. Public libraries serve as a stabilizing structure for many military families moving about with young children. I wasn't the only mom who put "check out the library" at the top of the new arrival To Do list. The lay of the land is different in every one, but kids feel more grounded when they track down their favorite books again--just like back home. Also, my first real job was working in a particularly homey university library. The job itself was easy, but working in the presence of all that knowledge sparked a sense of awe.

But beyond books, the public library remains a vital community resource, a place to go and hear an author speak, undertake research, or enroll in a class or a workshop. There are plenty of people whose lifelong learning plans involve simply and quietly putting new information into their brains through reading. Even if housed in a building that looks tired and dated, most libraries have kept pace with technology, putting electronic access to entire collections into our hands. Larger cities often feature special libraries, such as Chicago's independent research library, The Newberry, that dates back to 1887 and offers adult education programs and seminars on varied subjects, such as Edwardian Passions and

The Philosophy of Anxiety. University libraries might not permit books to circulate to nonstudents, but they typically welcome the public and allow access to reading rooms and collections.

Those looking for some guidance in selecting readings as a means of learning might check out Open Syllabus Explorer (explorer.opensyllabusproject.org/). The site lists books assigned via the syllabi of more than a million college and university courses around the U.S.

I admit it took me a while to learn there was much more to YouTube (www.youtube.com) than comedic videos that popped up from emailed links from friends and colleagues. The site features countless posts with instructional material. Poking around the site, I've discovered how to etch a figure 8 into the ice on figure skates; how to get a nice easy golf swing; and how to stroke a brush full of oil paints onto a canvas to create a realistic image of water, ripples, and reflections. But also available are types of mini-lectures from professors, such as the thoughtful little posting of Florida International University faculty member Campbell McGrath on how to write a poem.

Though there is nothing like a few precious minutes of unstructured time simply to think or simply to be in the moment, bits of learning can also squeeze into those small slivers of time if so inclined. Commuting on trains, waiting in lines, or sitting in carpool provide pockets of opportunity. I am a fan of podcasts, downloaded onto my technological dinosaur, the "old-fashioned" ipod. I take these along when I'm walking the dog to hear lectures, discussions, and stories along the way. She's a small dog with tiny legs and makes frequent sniff stops so the going is slow enough for a lecture, sometimes two. The pace is particularly well suited to TED talks (www.ted.com/talks). What a treat to hear presentations of what it's like to peer into space or to listen to a positive perspective on making mistakes or to better understand the power of being an introvert. I've found other gems on NPR's Fresh Air (www.npr.org/programs/fresh-air/) and The Writing University (www.writinguniversity.org/). Since I believe fiction teaches us about life, I consider listening to stories a form of learning as well. I have found some great tales among PRI's Selected Shorts (www.feeds.feedburner.com/Selected-Shorts) and the New Yorker Fiction (http://www.newyorker.com/podcast). I found these lectures and stories to be great supplemental material while studying for my MFA as well.

These are but a few of the countless resources out there to support a continued pursuit of knowledge. There are infinite ways to learn. I hope this collection of stories will inspire others to continue their own paths of learning with renewed vigor or perhaps spark a new educational endeavor in the future.

Thanks to the generous scholars who shared their experiences for this project and for showing the world that we are never too old to learn.

Works Cited

"Aspiring Docs," *AAMC Students, Applicants, and Residents,* Association of American Medical Colleges, (https://students-residents.aamc.org/choosing-medical-career/medical-careers/aspiring-docs/).

Haynie, Devon, "7 Warning Signs an Online Degree is a Scam," *U.S. News and World Report*, June 9, 2015. (https://www.usnews.com/education/online-education/articles/2015/06/09/7-warning-signs-an-online-degree-is-a-scam).

"Physician Shortages to Worsen Without Increases in Residency Training," *Tomorrow's Doctors, Tomorrow's Cures, Association of American Medical Colleges.* (https://www.aamc.org/download/153160/data/physician_shortages_to_worsen_without_increases_in_residency_tr.pdf).

Terkel, Studs, *Working: People Talk About What They Do All Day and How They Feel About What They Do*, The New Press, New York, 1972.

About the Author

Susan Sarver's writing has appeared in various anthologies, journals, magazines, and newspapers, including *The Christian Science Monitor, Portland Review,* and *Reader's Digest.* She holds an MFA in creative writing from Oregon State University-Cascades and lives in the high desert of Central Oregon.

Susan became interested in the subject of this work after returning to college at the age of ... let's just say one appropriate for this title.

Made in the USA
Lexington, KY
14 October 2018